CARING FOR
AUSTRALIAN WILDLIFE

CARING FOR AUSTRALIAN WILDLIFE

The management of sick, injured and orphaned native animals

by Sharon White

Photography by Martin Sauvarin

*with additional photographs by Rosemary Booth,
Jonathon and John Hanger, Mike Langford, Randy Larcombe,
Mitch Reardon, Angela Spencer and Peter White*

Illustrations by Murray Frederick

Published by Australian Geographic Pty Ltd
PO Box 321, Terrey Hills NSW 2084, Australia
Phone: (02) 9473 6777, fax (02) 9473 6701

First published 1997
Reprinted 1998, 2002

Managing Director: Ken Rosebery
Managing Editor, Books: Averil Moffat

Editor: Ken Eastwood
Design and Art Direction: Moyna Smeaton, Concept Press
Production Manager: Valerie Reed
Copy Editor: Frank Povah
Editorial Assistants: Joanne Diver, Susan McCreery

Printed in Hong Kong by South China Printing Company

National Library of Australia Cataloguing-in-Publication Data:
        White, Sharon, 1958 – .
        Caring for Australian Wildlife: a practical guide to the captive management
        of Australian native animals
        Bibliography.
        Includes index.
        ISBN 1 86276 021 7.
1. Zoology – Australia. 2. Captive wild animals – Australia. 3. First aid for animals. 4.
Animal handling – Australia. 5. Animal housing – Australia. I. Australian Geographic
Pty Ltd. II. Title.
        591.994

Acknowledgements
For their assistance with this book, Sharon White thanks: Rosie Booth for her
generous contribution; colleagues in Wildcare, especially Eleanor Hanger, Gail Gipp
and wildlife veterinarian Jonathon Hanger; Holly Peyton-Smith for the initial, detailed
reference illustrations; Helen George, Brian Rich, Sonya Stanvic, Linda Collins, Janet
Bronk, Carole Green, Greg Czechura and Marian Bangay for their professional advice;
and Neil Charles, Tania Carter, Penny Wilson, Sharon Griffiths, Bev O'Haire, Vicki
Pender, Currumbin Sanctuary and Fleays Wildlife Park, south-east Queensland, for
assistance with photography. Sharon would also like to thank her husband Pete for
all his help and support.

Contents

QUICK REFERENCE CHART

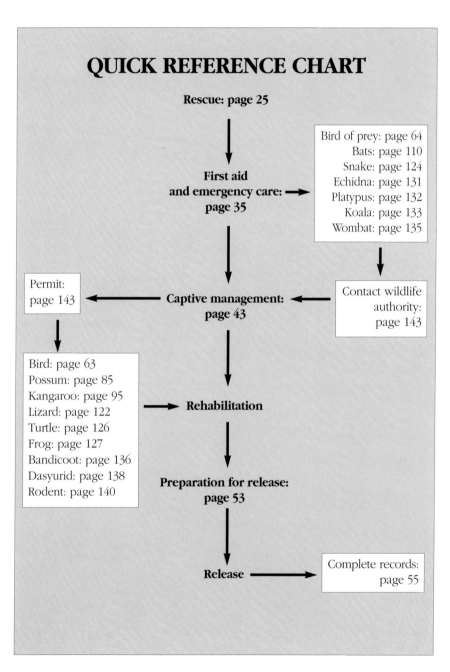

Rescue: page 25

First aid and emergency care: page 35 →

Bird of prey: page 64
Bats: page 110
Snake: page 124
Echidna: page 131
Platypus: page 132
Koala: page 133
Wombat: page 135

Permit: page 143 ← **Captive management: page 43** ← Contact wildlife authority: page 143

Bird: page 63
Possum: page 85
Kangaroo: page 95
Lizard: page 122
Turtle: page 126
Frog: page 127
Bandicoot: page 136
Dasyurid: page 138
Rodent: page 140

→ **Rehabilitation**

Preparation for release: page 53

Release → Complete records: page 55

Foreword

Australians are extremely fortunate to live in a country with so many wilderness areas and such wonderfully diverse wildlife. But each year thousands of native animals throughout the country are killed or injured by the activities of humans. Road trauma, predation by domestic pets and habitat destruction are common causes of injury and death. Less frequent but more devastating are major disasters such as bushfires and oil spills. Then there are the insidious and often unrecognised effects of environmental pollution.

Fortunately, part of what makes us human is our preparedness to consider the welfare of other species with which we share our environment.

Almost every Australian family will be confronted with a wildlife rescue situation at some time. Although nearly all rescued animals are common species, they are deserving of a genuine attempt to return them to their habitat or to humanely end their suffering if they cannot be released.

This book will help people rescue an animal safely and care for it until they can obtain professional help. It provides sound practical advice to encourage everyone to develop a responsible and caring attitude towards our wildlife.

The thoughtful text, in which Sharon White demonstrates her ability as a teacher and wildlife carer, explains principles for beginners and provides tips and reference information for more experienced carers. Essential facts can be gleaned with a quick glance at each excellent illustration, photograph or table.

Sharon has shared with us her respect for Australian wildlife and her many years of experience as a successful and dedicated wildlife carer so that we may all try harder to preserve Australia's natural wonders. In the end our own survival will depend on it.

Rosemary Booth
Wildlife veterinarian

Introduction

This comprehensive manual, an introduction to wildlife rehabilitation, provides simple and concise guidelines for the care of sick, injured and orphaned wildlife.

Many native animals come into care as a direct result of "human progress", so I believe we have a moral obligation to provide them with the best possible care and attention. An injured or orphaned animal left alone in the wild has very little chance of surviving. By taking it into care we can give it a second chance at life.

The aim of rehabilitating wildlife is to return it to the wild when it is strong, healthy and able to fend for itself. Unfortunately, so many native animals just don't survive in captivity – there is more to looking after them than most people realise.

The first half of this book outlines the principles involved in caring for Australian native animals. Practical advice is given on rescuing wildlife and providing emergency care, as well as detailing more sensitive issues such as euthanasia. The second half provides detailed information on the specific needs of these animals, such as their food and housing requirements. A glossary at the back of the book explains unfamiliar terms.

This book has a place in every home and will provide a handy reference guide for all wildlife emergencies.

Sharon White

The product of millions of years of evolution, rainforest provides an abundance of food and shelter for many Australian native animals. Environments such as this are our natural heritage and must be preserved – no amount of dedication from wildlife carers will save an animal species whose habitat has been destroyed.

PART ONE

CHAPTER ONE
WILDLIFE ECOLOGY

*Defines native wildlife and explores the close
relationship between the natural environment and
its plants and animals.*

Australian wildlife is made up of animals from two distinct groups:

Native species, which have evolved in Australia over a long period of time, include monotremes (platypuses and echidnas), marsupials (quolls, bilbies, koalas, possums, kangaroos, etc.), birds (emus, seabirds, raptors, honeyeaters, parrots, etc.), amphibians (tree frogs, burrowing frogs, etc.), reptiles (crocodiles, turtles, snakes, lizards), bats (flying-foxes, blossom-bats, insectivorous bats, etc.) and rodents (water-rats, tree-rats, rock-rats, native mice, etc.).

Introduced species, which are animals that have found their way into Australia in relatively recent times, include herbivorous mammals (rabbits, hares, cattle, sheep, goats, etc.), carnivorous mammals (foxes, dogs, cats), omnivorous mammals (pigs, rats, mice, etc.), birds (sparrows, feral pigeons, chickens, ostriches, peacocks, etc.) and amphibians (cane toads).

*Introduced hunters such as the European red fox
have had a major impact on Australian wildlife,
contributing to the extinction of some native species.
Foxes also compete for food and shelter with
native predators such as the
spotted-tailed quoll.*

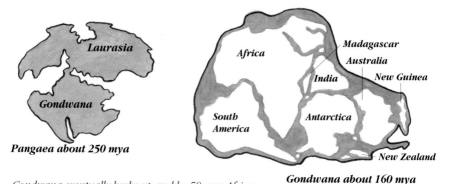

Gondwana eventually broke up and by 50 mya Africa,
Madagascar, India and New Zealand had separated, leaving
South America, Antarctica and Australia still joined.

THE PASSAGE OF TIME

It's difficult to understand the progressive changes that have shaped our native wildlife without some knowledge of evolutionary theory.

Originally, all of Earth's continents were joined together, forming the super-continent called Pangaea. About 225 million years ago (mya) Pangaea began to break in two, forming a northern continent, Laurasia, and a southern continent, Gondwana.

Gondwana originally held within it the land masses that we know today as Africa, India, Madagascar, New Zealand, South America, Antarctica and Australia. Gondwana's first animals were insects, primitive frogs, fish and reptiles. Dinosaurs and other giant reptiles ruled the continent until about 65 mya. Ancient birds and mammals evolved from the early reptiles.

Australia, still joined to New Guinea, separated from Gondwana about 35 mya and slowly drifted northwards. Lush rainforest covered much of the continent. Completely isolated, the existing animals had to continually adapt to changing conditions, especially the fluctuating climate. Over time they came to fill a variety of ecological niches. Our monotremes, marsupials, most of our birds, frogs, crocodiles and turtles have almost certainly evolved from these early creatures.

Around 20 mya the Australian continent drifted close to South-East Asia, allowing animals of Asian origin to enter Australia. The climate at this stage was very dry so the vegetation changed. Eucalypts, acacias and grasslands spread across the continent. South-East Asian animals such as bats, lizards, snakes and rodents adapted well to these new conditions.

Dingoes were introduced from South-East Asia about 4000 years ago, probably by Asian fishermen.

During the past 200 years many animals found their way into Australia for various reasons. Some were introduced for sport (rabbit, hare, fox, deer), others for food (cattle, sheep, pig, chicken), transport (horse, donkey, camel), work or companionship (cat, dog) or for fibre (sheep, goat). A few, such as the cane toad, were introduced to control pests. Others were introduced unintentionally (house mouse, black and brown rat).

THE IMPORTANCE OF HABITAT

A habitat is simply the place where an animal lives. It must provide all the basic requirements needed for an animal to survive, such as food, water and shelter.

Australia has many different types of habitat, including wetland, rainforest, eucalypt forest, heathland, grassland and desert. The plants in each habitat supply food and shelter for the animals. The wildlife, in turn, benefits the natural environment in many ways: controlling insect pests, pollinating flowers, dispersing seeds, pruning foliage and fertilising soil.

The key to the survival of native wildlife is the protection of its natural habitat.

Permanent wetlands provide reliable water for wildlife, especially in times of drought. Swamps and marshes also provide habitat for a range of native animals including waterfowl and wading birds. Islands of vegetation give birds protection from terrestrial predators.

Kookaburras inhabit open forests and woodlands, living in small family groups within well-defined territories. They strongly defend their domains and will generally attack "foreign" kookaburras found within their boundaries. For this reason, a kookaburra in care should be returned to its original territory within three weeks to improve its chances of survival.

THE BALANCE OF NATURE

The food supplied by nature provides the perfect balance of nutrients required by animals to live and breed successfully. When humans regularly feed wildlife with artificial food, they upset this balance.

The following examples show how artificial feeding can have a detrimental effect on native animals.

The **rainbow lorikeet's** natural diet is nectar, pollen, insects, manna and honeydew. If the bird is fed an artificial diet of bread, sugar and water – low in protein and deficient in many vitamins and minerals – its immune system is compromised and it becomes more susceptible to disease.

The **kookaburra's** natural diet of whole lizards, frogs, mice, birds and insects is high in calcium. Kookaburras need calcium to grow strong bones. If they're fed an artificial diet of mincemeat and meat scraps – low in calcium – their young are born with weak bones or bone deformities.

UPSETTING THE BALANCE

Nature's perfect balance allows a variety of animals to share any given habitat. If one species, say the kookaburra, is handfed regularly, its population increases due to the extra food provided. As a result, a larger number of kookaburras will prey on the young of the smaller birds that live in the area. Eventually the smaller birds will depart to seek a place where they can successfully raise their young, leaving behind only a large population of kookaburras.

ATTRACTING WILDLIFE NATURALLY

Ideally, we should strive to live in harmony with our native animals and enjoy watching them foraging for food and interacting. There are many ways to attract wildlife to your home other than by providing artificial foods. Here are a few simple ways by which you can provide natural food, water and shelter for native animals in your own backyard:

- Plant native trees and flowering shrubs to provide wildlife with a variety of natural food and shelter.
- Put bird baths and ponds in your garden, adding beauty, supplying water and attracting insects.
- Place wooden nesting-boxes in trees to encourage wildlife to sleep and breed close by.
- Leave clumps of undisturbed vegetation in secluded areas of the garden away from domestic pets.
- Leave an outside light on at night to attract an abundance of insects for nocturnal wildlife.
- Let the wildlife take care of the insects around your garden instead of using chemical deterrents.

Possums like to sleep in dark places. A strong wooden box mounted more than 4 m above the ground in a tree – preferably without damaging the plant – is ideal. Such boxes provide possums, like this pair of mountain brushtails, with a safe place to shelter.

15

OUR FRAGILE ECOSYSTEM

It is important to understand that we live within a complex ecosystem comprising plants, animals and the natural environment. Our native plants and animals have evolved together over a long period of time, and depend on each other for survival. The balance of nature is an essential part of this process.

The way in which we care for our native wildlife today will definitely influence its survival in the future.

PHOTOS: ANGELA SPENCER

Possums, gliders, microbats and birds shelter in tree hollows (left). Unfortunately it takes up to 200 years for some trees to develop suitable hollows, so it is absolutely crucial that old trees (below) are preserved. Some animal species' survival ultimately depends on people who work to protect these natural habitats.

People seeking to conserve precious habitats can start in their own backyards. A shallow birdbath set in the shade – and inaccessible to cats – is a valuable asset to any garden. Flowering plants such as wattles, bottlebrushes, banksias, tea-trees and grevilleas provide nectar and pollen for gliders, birds and megabats. Possums and koalas will eat eucalypt leaves and native grasses will attract wallabies and bandicoots.

17

PETER WHITE

As Earth's human population increases, it's inevitable that natural environments will be cleared to make way for new housing (above). With careful planning though, developers may choose to keep valuable "wildlife corridors" on their estates. These corridors are vital for the safe movement of animals from one large uncleared area to another, which in turn is critical in ensuring genetic diversity. Developers may also find that many people would prefer to live in estates where natural habitats have been retained and native animals continue to survive.

CHAPTER TWO
THE EFFECTS OF HUMANKIND

Problems facing native wildlife today.

Humans have altered the balance of nature in many ways and caused most of the problems our wildlife experiences. This is why many Australian animals now need human care.

ENVIRONMENTAL PROBLEMS

Habitat destruction is by far the largest threat to the survival of our native animals. Natural vegetation is destroyed to make way for developments such as housing estates, roads and railways, farms, industry, shopping centres and golf courses.

With their homes destroyed, native animals struggle to survive. Their supply of natural food disappears along with their shelter from predators and the elements. While the area is being cleared, many animals flee to neighbouring bush regions, leaving behind their vulnerable, dependent young. Homeless animals try to integrate into the surrounding areas, but may need to battle with animals already living there, competing for available food and shelter. It's these creatures that come into care due to their poor condition.

Poisoning is another threat to our wildlife. Humans have introduced a combination of poisonous concoctions into the natural environment. Animals can be poisoned by ingesting food or water that has been contaminated with chemicals such as herbicides, pesticides and fertilisers. Poisoning can also occur when animals inhale toxic fumes from the chemicals that pollute their environment.

Animals need our help after swallowing, or becoming entangled in, human rubbish such as plastic bags, fishing line or fishhooks. Sewage and industrial waste entering our waterways can also cause problems. Oil spills, in particular, have the potential to contaminate vast areas, affecting huge numbers of wildlife.

Bushfires are often called natural disasters, but in many instances the fires are deliberately lit by humans. Animals are often brought into care suffering smoke inhalation and burns. Care must be taken when returning these animals to their original habitat because food and shelter will be in short supply until the bush regenerates.

ACCIDENTS

Most injured and orphaned wildlife comes into care as a direct result of colliding with **motor vehicles**. The animals may be crossing the road to forage for food, search for a mate, look for new territory or escape from predators.

Streetlights and car headlights attract insects to the roads and nocturnal insectivores such as tawny frogmouths can be so intent on catching their dinner that they are oblivious to the danger.

After a collision with a motor vehicle, animals may suffer from injuries such as shock, concussion, bruising, broken bones, internal damage and severe bleeding. Although these accidents are often fatal, healthy marsupial young, such as possums and wallabies, can sometimes be found inside the pouch of severely injured or even dead mothers.

Lawn-mowers and powered edge-trimmers cause many accidents to ground-dwelling animals such as lizards, snakes and echidnas. The animal is usually hidden in long grass.

Birds often come into care after flying into **windows**. They are usually found in a dazed condition lying on the ground near the accident site. Stunned birds are vulnerable to attacks by other animals, especially dogs and cats. They need a safe place to recover from their ordeal. Most can be released within 24 hours.

OTHER PROBLEMS

Native animals are often attacked by other native wildlife. For example, eagles prey on rodents, birds and the smaller marsupials. This is part of the natural food chain and should not be a reason for wildlife carers to become involved.

However, attacks by **dogs and cats** are a common reason injured animals come into care. The risk of infection from these injuries is high, so veterinary attention is required immediately.

Domestic dogs and cats should be confined to their own properties and not allowed to wander. Cat owners should attach bells to their cats' collars and keep cats inside at night.

Despite good intentions, **human interference** can also cause problems. For example, when a young bird takes its first tentative flight, it may fall to the base of the nest tree. When finding a fledgling all alone, many humans feel compelled to intervene and bring it in for care. However, the parent birds are usually nearby and will continue to feed and

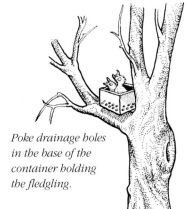

Poke drainage holes in the base of the container holding the fledgling.

Many nocturnal marsupials are killed by vehicles on country roads. It's always worthwhile to stop in a safe place, pull the animal off the road and check for live young. It's surprising just how many healthy joeys are rescued from the pouches of dead mothers.

It's very sad to see native animals being killed by dogs or cats. Although these pets are usually well fed, their natural hunting instincts make them a major threat to wildlife. Unfortunately many attacks occur when people entice wildlife into their backyards but fail to restrain their pets.

Electrocution is a seasonal problem for flying-foxes, which usually give birth to a single youngster in spring. New mothers carry their offspring vast distances every night as they forage for food. Burdened with the extra weight of their young, they often stop to rest on a powerline. If their wings make contact with a second wire they are killed instantly, but remarkably their young often survive. Ask the local electricity authority to rescue orphans.

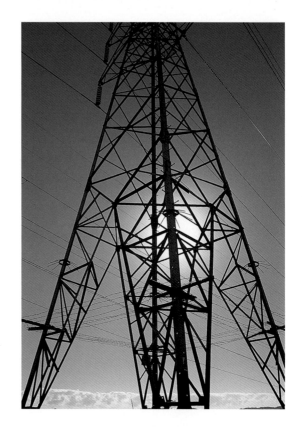

protect their young. They know that their offspring will gradually improve flight skills with practice. If you feel the bird is in immediate danger on the ground, secure a small container to the lower branches of the tree and place the fledgling inside.

Artificial diets are a common problem for birds that have become partial to feeding from trays. Some become totally dependent on this food and don't bother to find any natural food themselves. The artificial food may not contain the correct balance of nutrients to keep the bird healthy, so they become susceptible to disease.

Shooting of native animals can occur. This may be to protect crops, to help control large populations, or for resources such as food, fur, skins, etc. In some instances, mothers are killed and the young are found alive but orphaned.

Electrocution kills many Australian animals each year. Overhead powerlines provide a convenient resting place for animals such as birds, flying-foxes and possums. However, if an animal stretches out and makes contact with a second wire, it is killed instantly. Baby flying-foxes and possums are often seen, still alive, hanging off their dead mothers on powerlines. The nearest electricity authority should be contacted immediately. They will arrange to have the animal removed.

With its legs and body entwined in fishing line and a fishhook firmly embedded in its beak, this seagull faces a grim future. All attempts at rescuing it failed. By the time such individuals are captured they may be too weak to survive.

This X-ray clearly shows the fishing line, steel trace and fishhook that a saw-shelled turtle has swallowed. Turtles are commonly found with fishhooks firmly lodged inside their mouths. Unless the hook can be easily cut or removed, it's recommended that you consult a vet.

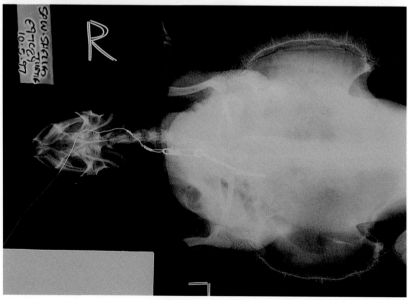

23

ANGELA SPENCER

Dodging suburban dangers is a risky business for many native animals – shrinking habitat, wandering dogs and cats and fast cars make survival a constant struggle. Before being rescued by an experienced snake handler, this carpet python was enjoying the sunshine and soaking up the road's warmth, completely oblivious to the commotion it was causing. It was relocated to nearby scrub.

CHAPTER THREE
RESCUE TECHNIQUES

*Describes the methods used to rescue, capture,
handle and transport wildlife.*

Wildlife carers are often required to go out and rescue native animals in distress.
Most of the basic rescue equipment needed can be found around the home.

RESCUE EQUIPMENT

• **Cardboard boxes**, lined with newspaper and punctured with ventilation
holes, can be used to confine most wildlife. Dark-coloured cotton **pillowcases**
can be used to capture and confine small animals such as possums, orphaned
joeys, lizards and snakes.

• **Towels and blankets** are useful when capturing animals or restraining those
that bite or scratch. Folded towels can also be used for bedding and blankets
for warmth.

• **Gloves**, although useful, should be used with discretion as they may harm
some animals. Disposables are ideal for messy situations, cotton gloves can
prevent scratches and heavy-duty ones can protect the carer from bites.

• **Scissors** can help free animals from entanglement.

• **Torches** are helpful at night and when looking inside tree hollows or other
dark places.

• Optional extras include a **net** for capturing small animals like birds, small bats
and frogs, and a **pet carry-cage** with metal latches for secure confinement and
transportation.

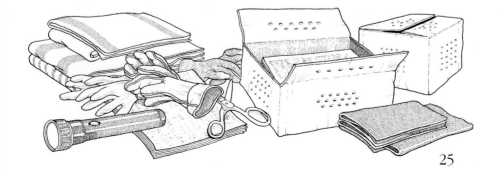

25

RESCUE PROCEDURE

Keep the basic equipment in the boot of your car ready for emergencies. If you receive a call about an animal in distress, make sure you have clear directions on its location and also take the name and telephone number of the contact person in case of difficulties. Stay calm and don't speed to the rescue site. Do not endanger your own life while attempting to save an animal.

Remove dead animals from the road because they could attract other animals to the site and cause another accident.

FURLESS JOEY RESCUE

If you have to remove a live infant marsupial from its dead mother's pouch, be aware that it can be firmly attached to the teat. Place your fingers on either side of the joey's mouth and very slowly and carefully slide the teat out. Do not forcibly pull the teat from the joey's mouth. If unable to extract the teat gently, cut the teat close to the lining of the pouch. Scoop the joey out, wrap it securely and keep it warm.

Tiny joeys have specialised needs and it is essential to seek further advice from an experienced carer as soon as possible.

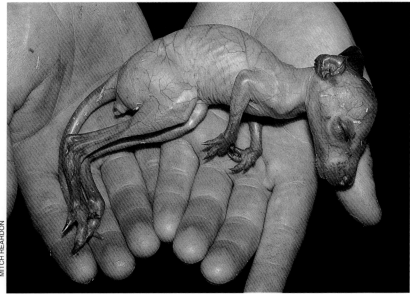

MITCH REARDON

When rescuing an echidna, firmly grasp its back feet and lift it off the ground. It will uncurl and stretch out. Try to hold the animal so its soft-furred underbelly, rather than its spines, faces you. Place it headfirst into a deep plastic bin. Cardboard boxes are not suitable as echidnas can burrow through them.

RESTRAINING WILDLIFE

The following methods will help when capturing, handling and transporting sick, injured or orphaned wildlife. Many large animals, such as emus, adult kangaroos and crocodiles can be extremely dangerous and difficult to handle, even when sick or injured. Seek expert assistance if required.

HANDLING WITH SAFETY

Capturing, restraining and handling wild animals can be very stressful for all concerned. The procedure is a lot smoother when handlers work quickly and efficiently – firm and confident in their approach, but gentle in their manner.

Take a minute or two to plan the capture and have all your equipment handy, including the holding facility. If possible, approach quietly from behind, then be swift and accurate in capturing the animal, taking care not to injure it further. Don't allow birds to flap their wings frantically while they are being restrained. Be cautious of sharp teeth, beaks and claws. Animals will use these to defend themselves, so hold them with these parts facing away from your body. Once captured, confine the animal securely. Most animals quieten down considerably once the head is covered and their movements are restricted.

Ducks are relatively easy to handle and often come into care, so it's important to become familiar with their needs. As with all birds, ensure the wings are held firmly against the animal's body to prevent flapping and further injury.

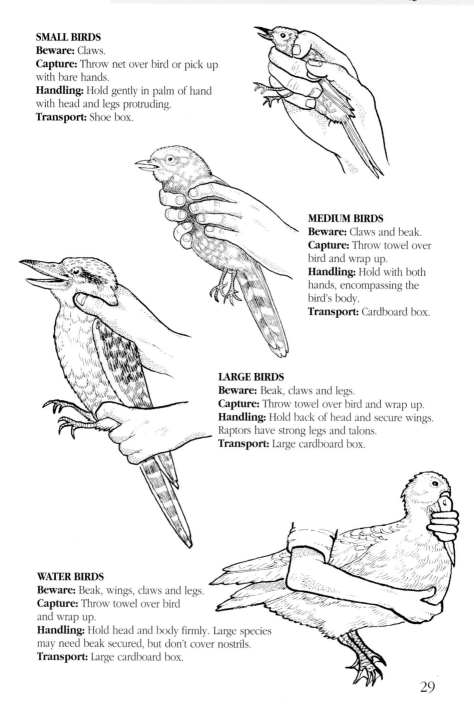

SMALL BIRDS
Beware: Claws.
Capture: Throw net over bird or pick up with bare hands.
Handling: Hold gently in palm of hand with head and legs protruding.
Transport: Shoe box.

MEDIUM BIRDS
Beware: Claws and beak.
Capture: Throw towel over bird and wrap up.
Handling: Hold with both hands, encompassing the bird's body.
Transport: Cardboard box.

LARGE BIRDS
Beware: Beak, claws and legs.
Capture: Throw towel over bird and wrap up.
Handling: Hold back of head and secure wings. Raptors have strong legs and talons.
Transport: Large cardboard box.

WATER BIRDS
Beware: Beak, wings, claws and legs.
Capture: Throw towel over bird and wrap up.
Handling: Hold head and body firmly. Large species may need beak secured, but don't cover nostrils.
Transport: Large cardboard box.

29

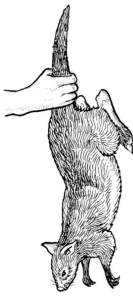

POSSUMS AND GLIDERS
Beware: Teeth and claws.
Capture: Use pillowcase as a glove and scoop inside.
Handling: Hold back of head and base of tail firmly.
Transport: Pillowcase inside box.

KANGAROOS AND WALLABIES
Beware: Claws, hind legs and teeth.
Capture: Throw blanket over kangaroo and wrap up.
Handling: Hold base of tail and support chest, lift
and place headfirst inside bag.
Transport: Pillowcase for orphans,
large hessian sack for adults.

WOMBATS
Beware: Teeth, claws and aggressive nature.
Capture: Throw blanket over wombat or coerce into box.
Handling: Hold under armpits from behind, lift and place
in crate. You need to be strong.
Transport: Large wooden crate.

KOALAS
Beware: Claws and teeth.
Capture: Throw blanket over koala and wrap up.
Handling: With one hand firmly holding the
scruff of the neck and the other supporting the
rump, lift and place in box.
Transport: Large wooden box with a vertical
branch secured inside.

ECHIDNAS
Beware: Spines.
Capture: Tap the echidna's forehead with your fingertip and its hind legs will dart out.
Handling: Grab back feet and lift up. Place head first into bin.
Transport: Deep plastic garbage bin.

PLATYPUSES
Beware: Males have poisonous spur on hind leg.
Capture: Throw towel over platypus and wrap up.
Handling: Hold base of tail from behind, lift and place inside box.
Transport: Wooden box.

INSECTIVOROUS BATS
Beware: Teeth.
Capture: Throw net over bat or pick up with gloved hands.
Handling: Hold gently in palm of hand, head protruding.
Transport: Pillowcase, tied securely.

SMALL MARSUPIALS AND RODENTS
Beware: Teeth and claws.
Capture: Use pillowcase as a glove and scoop inside.
Handling: Hold back of head and support body.
Transport: Pillowcase inside box.

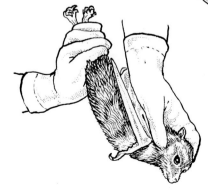

FLYING-FOXES
Beware: Teeth, claws and wings.
Capture: Wrap towel firmly around body, securing head and wings. Leave legs free.
Handling: Wearing heavy-duty gloves, hold feet and head securely.
Transport: Deep cardboard box, poke branch through side of box, allow bat to hang.

31

SNAKES
Beware: Mouth.
Capture: Best left to experts. Reptile hooks and snake nets are usually required.
Handling: With caution, hold head securely and support body.
Transport: Calico bag or pillowcase, securely tied.

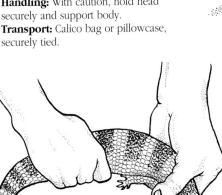

LIZARDS
Beware: Teeth, claws and tail.
Capture: Throw towel over lizard or coerce into box.
Handling: Hold back of head and support body. Large species need tail and legs secured.
Transport: Pillowcase inside box.

FROGS
Beware: Toxic skin secretions.
Capture: Throw net over frog or pick up with wet hands.
Handling: Hold with wet hands cupped around frog.
Transport: Wet pillowcase.

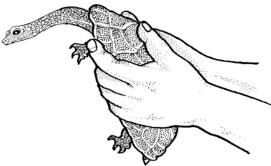

FRESHWATER TURTLES
Beware: Claws and mouth.
Capture: Throw towel over turtle or pick up with bare hands.
Handling: Hold edge of shell with both hands.
Transport: Cardboard box.

Capturing a wallaby usually requires at least two people. While one holds an open sack low to the ground, the other should approach the animal quietly from behind, firmly grabbing the base of its tail then quickly lifting it, placing it headfirst into the bag. Care should be taken to ensure no-one is struck by the powerful hind limbs.

TRANSPORTING WILDLIFE

All wildlife must be securely confined for transportation. Tape the cardboard box down or tie the end of the pillowcase. Boxes can be secured with seat belts in the back seat of a car. Leave a car window open for extra ventilation.

Don't be tempted to put the animal in the boot – it could be affected by toxic fumes from the car exhaust.

Drive straight home where you can immediately carry out first aid and emergency care.

33

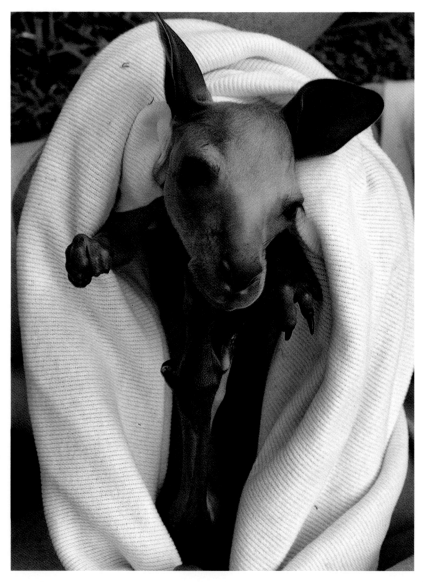

Lucky to be alive, this eastern grey kangaroo joey was involved in a road accident in which his mother was killed. He was placed inside a cotton pouch and treated for shock, his only injuries being superficial grazing down one leg, and bruising. With specialised care, joeys as young as this can be rehabilitated and returned to the wild.

CHAPTER FOUR
FIRST AID AND EMERGENCY CARE

The first 24 hours of care are most important when caring for sick, injured and orphaned wildlife. Here are steps to be taken during this critical period.

Most sick, injured and orphaned wildlife will be suffering from shock due to the trauma associated with a road accident, dog or cat attack, concussion, burns, severe injury, poisoning, etc. An animal in shock needs urgent attention.

It is essential to provide these animals with warmth and a safe, quiet place to recover. Once they have warmed up they should be given high-energy fluids.

Do not feed an animal in shock. Food should only be supplied after the animal has perked up following administration of high-energy fluids.

When providing emergency care for wildlife, try to reduce stress at all times.

FIRST-AID PRINCIPLES

Although basic first aid and emergency care can initially be applied by the carer, prompt veterinary assistance should always be sought. Some animals such as monotremes (platypus and echidna) and reptiles have special needs, and should be passed on to experienced carers as soon as possible.

Bleeding

Severe bleeding must be stopped by applying pressure directly to the wound. Place a clean bandage firmly over the wound, treat the animal for shock and consult your veterinarian.

Breathing difficulties

Checking for body movement will help identify breathing difficulties. Airways must be clear and free of debris. When restraining wildlife take care not to block the airway.

Broken bones

Do not attempt to splint or strap broken bones by yourself. Wrap the animal in a clean cloth to avoid further injury, treat for shock and consult your vet.

Burns

Gradually cool burns using water or a cold compress. Gently wrap the area with a clean, wet cloth, then treat for shock and dehydration and consult your vet. Complications may include infection and smoke inhalation.

Dehydration

This can be treated with oral rehydration solutions such as Lectade or Vytrate (available from vet clinics), which replace lost fluids and electrolytes. Offer small drinks frequently during the first 24 hours, aiming to give the animal at least 15 per cent of its body weight in fluids during this time. In cases of severe dehydration consult your vet about intravenous fluids.

Hyperthermia and hypothermia

Mammals have a normal body (cloacal) temperature of 35–37 °C, birds 40–42 °C. To treat hyperthermia (heat stress), place the animal in a cool environment, gradually lowering its temperature using water, towels and fans. Stop when normal body temperature is reached and treat for dehydration. Hypothermia, or chill, can be treated by gradually warming the animal with a constant, artificial heat source (page 38). The animal should be given neither food nor water until normal body temperature is reached.

Oil contamination

Oil contamination in birds destroys the waterproofing and insulation of feathers and causes internal damage if oil is swallowed. On site, wipe the beak clean and prevent birds from ingesting extra oil by wrapping each bird in a soft cloth or poncho, keeping its head free. This will discourage it from preening until the feathers have been cleaned. Once home, gently wash the bird's feathers in a solution of mild dishwashing liquid and warm water until all oil is removed. Rinse the bird thoroughly and allow it to dry in sunlight. Treat for shock and consult your vet.

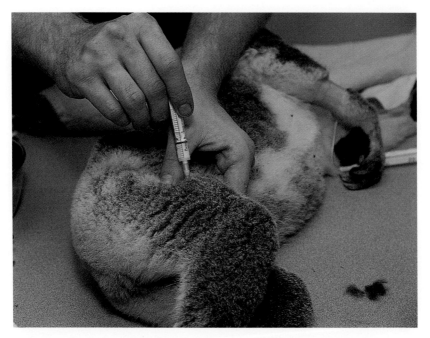

When injections are needed, they're usually administered by a vet after a full examination of the animal. Some carers may have to learn to give injections at home as part of an animal's treatment, but only under veterinary supervision. Carers need to understand that their job is rehabilitation – diagnosis and treatment should be left up to vets.

Parasites

Although these don't usually cause an emergency, they often go hand-in-hand with injury and disease. The added stress of a parasite burden can affect an animal's response to treatment, so it's always wise to eliminate them. External parasites such as fleas can be removed with a flea comb, ticks and maggots with tweezers, and lice and mites can be lightly sprayed with pyrethrin or dusted with carbaryl. If the animal has internal parasites, such as worms, keep a faecal specimen for examination by your vet, who will recommend an appropriate drench.

Poisoning

Symptoms of poisoning may include vomiting, incoordination, convulsions, paralysis, coma and death. Treat for shock and consult your vet.

37

Shock
Provide warmth and put the animal in a stress-free environment. Once warm, offer high-energy fluids.

Wounds
Minor wounds are best left alone to allow blood to clot. Contaminated wounds can be washed in warm, salty water – half a teaspoon of salt to 250 millilitres of warm water. Dog or cat bites that puncture skin permit bacteria to enter the bloodstream, so your vet should be consulted about antibiotics.

WARMTH

Animals in shock need instant warmth. Artificial warmth can be provided by a light bulb, hot-water bottle or electric heat pad.

Air temperature should always be monitored closely because overheating can be fatal. Keep a thermometer beside the animal and check it regularly.

You may find daytime temperatures are warm enough and artificial heating is needed only at night. Naturally, extra warmth will be required during the colder months of the year.

The heat source should ideally be positioned at one end of the housing to allow the animal to approach or move away from the warmth. Place a small dish of water between the heat source and the animal to increase the humidity.

Be guided by your own instincts when monitoring the temperature – if the animal is panting and hot to the touch, lower the temperature; if it's shivering and cold to the touch, raise it.

AIR TEMPERATURE GUIDE		
Birds	Sick/injured adults	26°C
	Feathered young	30°C
	Featherless young	36°C
Mammals	Sick/injured adults	26°C
	Furred young	28°C
	Furless orphans	32°C
	Platypuses/echidnas	25°C
Reptiles	Freshwater turtles	26°C
	Lizards/snakes	30°C

Vetrap – a colourful, elasticised bandage used extensively on wildlife – provides support to a damaged ligament in a royal spoonbill's hind toe (left). Vetrap's main advantage is that it doesn't stick to fur or feathers, but care must be taken to ensure it's not applied too tightly.

With an open wound on her chest from a collision with a car, this koala (below) looks very upset. Veterinary assistance was required, but she was eventually returned to the wild after making an excellent recovery.

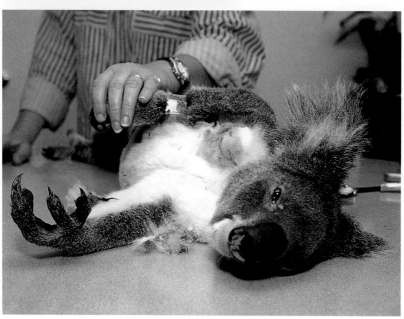

39

STRESS-FREE ENVIRONMENT

Animals in shock need peace and quiet – stress alone can kill them. As well as suffering the stress of injury, sickness or being orphaned, a captured animal faces extra stresses because it has lost its freedom, is housed in a strange environment, is confronted by unfamiliar sounds and smells and is not used to being handled by humans.

Dark and cosy housing provides distressed animals with a safe retreat. Keep this housing away from draughts, domestic pets and loud and unfamiliar noises such as TV and radio.

HIGH-ENERGY FLUIDS

Only give fluids to a warm animal. Offer small lukewarm drinks frequently.

One teaspoon of Glucodin mixed with 250 mL pre-boiled water is the easiest way to provide high-energy fluid to mammals and birds. Glucodin is available from most supermarkets and chemists.

High-energy fluids help stabilise the animal, combat dehydration, maintain body temperature and rest the stomach before different foods, such as artificial milk formulas, are introduced.

Sick or injured reptiles may need vitamin B complex and vitamin C supplements as well as rehydration therapy. These are best administered as subcutaneous injections by your vet.

VETERINARY ASSISTANCE

During the initial period of care it is important to assess the animal's condition. Observe the animal and record any information that may help the vet reach an accurate diagnosis.

When you approach your vet for assistance, be sure to telephone first, explaining your situation and asking for an appointment. Confine the animal securely for transportation to the clinic and go straight there.

Take all your recorded information. The vet may ask where and under what circumstances the animal was found, how long it has been in your care and what you've noticed about it.

Listen to the vet's advice and respect the diagnosis as final. Vets are the most qualified people to make a full health assessment of your animal. The decision to treat will take into consideration extent of injuries, chances of recovery and ability to survive when released.

All registered vets are legally required to relieve suffering in any animal, including natives. Most do not charge for this service.

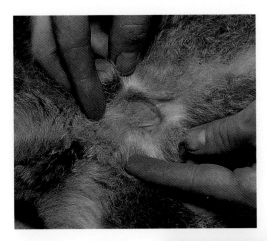

Checking the pouch for a joey is part of a vet's routine when examining an injured female marsupial like this koala. A newborn joey makes its way from the cloacal opening, up through the fur and into the warm, moist pouch where it attaches itself firmly to a teat. Snug and cosy inside this sterile, humid environment, the youngster will continue to grow and develop.

A warmed Glucodin-and-water drink provides instant energy to birds and mammals recovering from shock. An adult bird should be encouraged to drink the liquid by gently guiding its beak into a dish. Eye-droppers – not syringes – are good for orphaned birds. A bottle and teat can be used for marsupials.

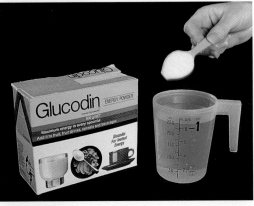

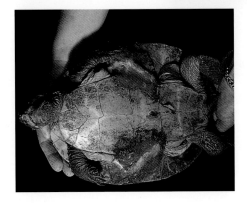

Epoxy resins and/or fibreglass should be used to repair all turtle-shell fractures, except minor chips around the edge. Single or multiple fractures of the hard shell may occur when freshwater turtles become road-accident victims. Even badly broken shells can be successfully treated if the animal is taken to a vet promptly.

41

Weighing this orphaned red-necked pademelon and taking its foot and tail measurements helped the carer estimate its age at 4.5 months. It's least stressful to weigh marsupial young and their pouch together, deducting the pouch's weight later – this joey weighed 310 g. Animals should be weighed at the same time each week to gain an accurate assessment of their progress. Wildlife carers should buy appropriate equipment including digital scales such as these, which are also useful when preparing milk formulas.

CHAPTER FIVE
CAPTIVE MANAGEMENT

*General principles involved in rehabilitating wildlife
and the benefits of mimicking nature in all aspects of
care and management.*

When you agree to care for a sick, injured or orphaned animal you are responsible for all aspects of its welfare. Many people are intrigued by our unique wildlife and the idea of looking after a native animal is very appealing.

However, the job is very demanding. A native animal is not a pet and the dedicated carer needs to be committed to providing its needs. A responsible wildlife carer should have access to suitable food, appropriate housing facilities, foster-caring equipment and should have good management skills.

The secret of successful wildlife rehabilitation is mimicking nature and providing natural conditions whenever possible. The aim is to release the animal back into the wild as a strong, healthy creature that is likely to survive.

IDENTIFICATION

First you must accurately identify the animal in your care. Use reference books and take particular note of physical features, size, shape and colour markings. Wildlife organisations (page 143) can also assist with identification.

Once identified, learn all about your animal and how it exists in the wild. Useful information may include what the animal eats, when it feeds and where it lives and sleeps. This extra knowledge will enable you to provide the right conditions for the animal in captivity.

NUTRITION

The best food for your native animal is the food that it eats in the wild. Try to provide as much natural food as you can because it will contain the right balance of nutrients.

Good nutrition is essential for recuperation from disease or injury, adequate growth and protection from disease while in captivity. Therefore, it is beneficial for carers to have a basic understanding of nutrition.

Quality identification books (above) help wildlife carers accurately identify the animal in their care so they can provide appropriate conditions and natural food during its rehabilitation. Native animals should be given a high percentage of natural food every day. For example, macropods such as this pademelon (below) generally emerge late in the afternoon to feed on native grasses and shrubs. In captivity they do best when housed in a near-natural environment with access to different types of native grasses. This natural diet can be supplemented with small portions of lucerne hay or kangaroo pellets.

JOHN HANGER

- **Protein** is used for growth, tissue repair, blood formation, reproduction and lactation. It is found in animal-based foods such as birds, mammals, reptiles, fish, insects, eggs and milk; and plant-based foods such as pollen, grasses, seeds, nuts, roots and leaves. Most creatures require some animal protein in their diet because plant protein is of a lesser quality.
- **Carbohydrate** is the main source of energy for many animals. It is found in plant-based foods such as grasses, seeds, grains, nectar, fruit and berries. Carbohydrate is muscle fuel – used for movement, digestion and breathing.
- **Fat** is the concentrated energy store for animals, containing twice as much energy as carbohydrate. It is found in animal-based foods and oilseeds such as linseed, rape, sunflower and safflower. Fat is used for energy, insulation and waterproofing.
- **Fibre** is the indigestible part of plant-based foods such as grains, seeds, grasses, leaves and fruits. It helps maintain normal bowel function.
- **Vitamins and minerals** are found in small amounts in most natural foods and are required every day to maintain good health. A prolonged deficiency in any of the required 30 vitamins and minerals will produce health problems. A vitamin-mineral supplement may be given to an animal in captivity, following the manufacturer's recommended dosage rates. Calcium can also be used in small amounts, especially for growing orphans, but it requires a proportional amount of phosphorus and the presence of vitamin D for proper assimilation.
- **Water** is needed for maintaining hydration and excreting waste. All animals require fresh, clean drinking water daily.

In the wild, animals feed from a large variety of natural foods and it is virtually impossible to offer this same range in captivity. However, most **commercial food supplements** contain the right balance of nutrients for specific animals. These supplements should be used in conjunction with the animal's natural food so that a well-balanced diet can be achieved. For further information on food-supplement suppliers refer to page 144.

There are many ways to gather **live food** for animals in captivity. Night-flying insects can be caught by turning an outside light on. Termites can be found in decayed timber, and aquatic insects and larvae can be scooped from ponds or dams. Look in the compost heap for insects and worms, and leave out over-ripe fruit to attract vinegar flies. Search foliage for scale, aphids, bugs and beetles.

Mealworms, crickets, earthworms, mice, etc., are available at pet shops and can be bred by the carer for a constant supply.

Rodent-breeding enclosures (above) can be set up in your own home, assuring you of a plentiful supply of furless baby mice, small furred mice or even large rats. Many carnivores eat rodents in their natural diet and, although rats and mice can be bought in bulk from pet shops, it's often cheaper for wildlife carers to breed their own.

Easy to keep clean and light to move, pet carry-cages (right) are perfect for transporting and housing wildlife. They come in different sizes to suit a variety of small mammals and birds.

HOUSING FACILITIES

In emergency situations, many items around the home can provide temporary housing for wildlife. All housing must be well ventilated.

Cardboard boxes suit a variety of wildlife. They are excellent for birds because cardboard minimises feather damage. **Polystyrene boxes** are good for aquatic animals and also for providing good insulation, helping to retain warmth. Large **garbage bins** with deep, smooth sides and tight-fitting lids can house lizards, snakes, echidnas and even koalas initially.

More permanent facilities are needed when you take on the responsibility of rehabilitating native animals. **Pet carry-cages** provide safe, secure housing and are suitable for orphans, small marsupials and rodents. **Cocky cages** are suitable for juvenile birds, possums, flying-foxes and convalescing animals. Small **wooden boxes** with a tight-fitting, fine-wire-mesh lid are ideal for insectivorous bats, lizards and snakes. **Fish tanks** with a similar lid suit frogs, freshwater turtles, lizards and snakes. They are also suitable for small carnivorous marsupials and native rodents.

Grouping marsupials together in a natural-like environment well away from domestic pets has many advantages. This swamp wallaby has free range of a large enclosure that resembles its natural habitat. Ferns and shrubs grow among the leaf litter and patches of native grasses are scattered throughout. A roofed enclosure for other nocturnal marsupials has been built within the run.

• **Aviaries** with natural branches for perches and native vegetation make excellent pre-release housing for birds, possums, koalas and flying-foxes.
• **Outside pens** with smooth, high sides can be used for burrowing animals such as wombats and echidnas, as long as the bottom is lined with heavy-duty wire mesh well below ground level.
• **Grassed enclosures** with high, wire fencing to stop predators and prevent escape are suitable for kangaroos and wallabies. Tussock grass and shrubs in the enclosure provide natural shelter.

All housing should imitate the animal's natural environment as much as possible. It must provide protection from the elements, have plenty of cover in which the animal can hide and be situated well away from domestic pets.

FOSTER-CARING EQUIPMENT

Equipment needed to care for sick, injured and orphaned wildlife in captivity includes:

Heat pad/hot-water bottle – to provide warmth.
Thermometer – to monitor temperature.
Cotton towels/woollen blankets – for bedding and warmth.
Inner/outer pouches – different sizes, made from natural fibres (no frayed edges or loose fibres).
Glucodin – for instant energy.
Lectade/Vytrate – oral rehydration solution.
Scales – for preparing milk formulas and weighing animals.
Reference books – for identifying native animals.
Food • natural such as grass, leaves, flowers, insects.
        • artificial such as milk formula, baby cereal, birdseed.
        • commercial food supplements.
Measuring cups and spoons – for correct food quantities.
Feeding utensils – bottles, teats, syringes, eye-dropper.
Bottlebrushes – to clean feeding utensils.
Antibacterial solution – to sterilise feeding utensils.
Tissues, paper towels – an endless supply.
Nappy wash – to sanitise bedding and pouches.
Sorbolene cream – for dry, chafed skin (without glycerine or vitamin E).
First-aid kit – tweezers, scissors, bandages, tape, iodine, safety pins, cotton wool, cotton tips.
Antibacterial soap – for cleaning hands, killing germs.

MANAGEMENT SKILLS

Good management skills are needed for the overall wellbeing of native animals while they are in captivity. The main factors vital for successful wildlife rehabilitation are:

• **Safety** – you must never put yourself or other people at risk while caring for native fauna. The animals must also be handled and housed in such a way as to protect them from further injuries or stress.

• **Good hygiene** in food preparation, the animal's housing and your own behaviour limits the amount of bacteria that can be passed on to an animal in care. Warm milk only once, discard leftover food, wipe food from the animal's mouth after handfeeding, sterilise feeding utensils used for tiny orphans, keep clean bottles and teats in the refrigerator, remove all uneaten food from cages and clean feed dishes thoroughly.

To prevent the spread of infectious diseases, isolate all new animals and clean and disinfect cages between occupants. Soak bedding and pouches in nappy wash, then wash, rinse thoroughly and hang them to dry in sunlight. Provide clean bedding after each feed because contaminated bedding is a haven for bacteria. Wash the animal with soap and water if it becomes soiled. Remove faeces from cages and enclosures every day.

Wash your own hands with antibacterial soap before and after handling each animal. Be aware of diseases that can be transmitted to humans and take precautions such as wearing gloves or burning contaminated bedding. Thoroughly clean any wounds resulting from animal bites or scratches.

Enjoying each other's company, these orphaned kangaroos have been transferred to a pre-release yard where they will become totally independent before being released back to the wild.

In many instances disease in captive animals is due to bad management. Native animals are more susceptible to disease when their immune system is weak. If you notice that your animal is sick, seek professional help sooner rather than later.

Healthy animals are active, alert and bright-eyed, groom themselves, maintain body temperature and have a good appetite. Sick animals may be lethargic and have dull eyes and no appetite; they may not bother to groom themselves and can't maintain normal body temperature.

• **Encouragement** is often needed for an animal to take an interest in life again. This could be as simple as encouraging grooming by gently brushing the fur of a convalescing marsupial or lightly spraying the feathers of a fledgling with water to encourage preening.

Orphans flourish once they have developed a special bond with their carer. Native animals respond better when there is only one carer who attends to their needs. This special bond is not to be confused with spoiling or becoming too emotionally involved with your animal. Orphans especially may need love and nurturing up to a point, but then they must be encouraged to become confident in their own right.

Some animals do much better when they are raised in a group. The close bond between animals of the same species provides the stimulation needed for their natural development. The social skills that they learn from living together can be of great benefit to them once released back into the wild.

• **Record-keeping** is essential. Initial information must include the exact place where the animal was found and the date the animal was rescued.

Weekly progress charts are vital for good management as they provide a detailed history of the animal's progress in care. If weight loss is recorded, you are alerted straight away and can rectify the cause immediately. Comments on the charts could include any changes in diet or faeces, unusual behaviour, health problems and medications.

Comprehensive records enable us to evaluate our personal methods of care, learn from past mistakes and improve our management skills.

WEEKLY PROGRESS CHART

Name of animal:

Species:

Sex:

Age:

Date	Weight	Comments

As this koala pauses for a moment to say goodbye, the smiles of its human friends say it all: what a privilege it is to rehabilitate these unique animals! Caring for them takes time and money, but the rewards are great – like the feeling of achievement when your animal is returned to its natural environment, ready to resume its life again. Fitted with a radio collar, this koala will be monitored over the next 12 months.

CHAPTER SIX
RELEASE INTO THE WILD

*Preparation needed to ensure native animals
have the best chance of survival when released
into the wild.*

The aim of caring for sick, injured and orphaned wildlife is to return them to the wild strong and healthy with the best chance of survival.

ASSESSMENT

A native animal must be totally independent before it can be released.

The animal should be physically fit and healthy, capable of finding natural food sources, accustomed to natural shelter (not just artificial bedding) and acclimatised to weather conditions. It should be familiar with its own species, preferring its own kind to human company, and alert to danger, hiding when alarmed.

RELEASE SITE

Release sites must have plenty of food, access to water and natural shelter. Beware of predators living nearby. A high number of predators will reduce the chance of your animal surviving.

Generally, a native animal should be released in the area where it was found – a rehabilitated animal is unlikely to survive in a completely different location. The type of food available, the habitat, climate and the predators it has learnt to avoid, all contribute to make the animal's original home the first choice for its release site.

Unfortunately, it's not always feasible to release an animal in its original home. The original site may be close to busy roads or in the middle of suburbia – the very reason the animal needed care in the first place. In these circumstances, animals can be relocated to a nearby area if the conditions appear suitable in every way.

PERMISSION TO RELEASE

It is necessary to obtain permission from your local wildlife authority before releasing a native animal into the wild. They can also arrange to have your animal marked before release with a leg band, ear tags or tattoo. If a marked animal is found at some future time, valuable information can be recorded, such as how long the animal survived before being found, its condition when found and the distance from the release site. This information can be used to evaluate methods of rehabilitation and release.

Permission must also be obtained from the owner of the release site. It is advisable to leave your phone number with them so you can be contacted if they notice anything unusual.

If you wish to release an animal in a national park you need permission from the ranger.

RIGHT TIME TO RELEASE

To increase its chance of survival, your animal should be released at the right time of day and in good weather. Nocturnal animals are best released at dusk and diurnal species at dawn. Summer is a good time to release because food is abundant.

With orphaned animals, find out at what age they become independent in the wild. Aim to release them when they would normally leave their mothers. Other animals are more tolerant of juveniles in the group at this time and it gives released animals a chance to adjust.

Migratory birds must be released at least one month before they are due to migrate. These birds need time in the wild to build up their flight muscles and to gain extra weight for their long journey. Otherwise they should remain in captivity until the species returns to your area next season. A general rule is to make sure the species you are releasing is seen living nearby at the time of release.

A migratory species, the dollarbird spends the winter in southern Asia and flies back to Australia to breed in spring. If these birds come into care, they should be rehabilitated and released before the end of summer. Otherwise they must remain in captivity over winter, then released in September, when the species returns to breed.

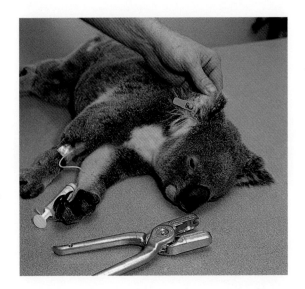

Koala populations are declining, so rescued and rehabilitated individuals are tagged before release. If they come into care again, the information gained about them may prove useful to wildlife authorities trying to solve management problems associated with wild populations.

RECORDS

After releasing your native animal, it is important to record the date, site, weight of the animal when released and tag or band number (if used). Keep all records of rehabilitated wildlife for future reference.

METHODS OF RELEASE

• **Hard release** is when a native animal is set free with no further support. It is suitable for animals that have been in captivity for only a short time.

• **Soft release** means setting a native animal free while providing a degree of support following the release. This could mean leaving food or shelter at the release site until the animal feels more confident in its new surroundings. This method is suitable for native animals that have been in captivity for a long time.

• **Self release** is a type of soft release that I've found successful, particularly when releasing possums. An aviary is situated in secluded natural bushland and the possums are placed in it before release. Artificial feeding is gradually withdrawn and natural food increased. Over time they adopt normal behaviour traits such as scent-marking their territory. Then the hatch is opened. The animals have the security of their own shelter (hollow log, nest-box, etc.) and a safe haven to return to should they need it. As they gain confidence in their new surroundings, they seek out natural shelters and mingle with their own kind. Eventually they move on to establish their own territory.

Large aviary-like enclosures hidden away in a bush environment (above) make ideal pre-release housing for many native animals. When the door is opened, most take off as soon as they can. Others, like this mountain brushtail possum (right), take their time, scurrying back to their retreat at the first sign of danger.

56

RULES OF THE BUSH

You are responsible for looking after a native animal only until it can fend for itself. Once fully rehabilitated, it is your moral obligation to set it free. It is wrong to believe that a native animal is better off spending the rest of its life in captivity just because you're afraid of what might happen to it when it is set free.

The rules of the bush are simple: strong and healthy animals survive; weak, sick and old animals perish.

All animals must eat to survive. In the wild, native predators such as eagles, owls, goannas, pythons and quolls may selectively remove the weak, sick and old animals from the community. This way nature provides its own quality control. The weaker animals become a food source and are therefore unable to pass their genes on to the next generation.

Introduced predators such as foxes, dogs and cats hunt and kill a wide range of birds, mammals and reptiles. In areas where these predators exist in large numbers, native animals struggle to survive.

Introduced herbivores such as rabbits and hares don't kill wildlife directly but destroy the natural vegetation, making it very difficult for our native wildlife to survive.

Native animals can become diseased for many reasons, including malnutrition, infection and injury. An animal carrying disease becomes an easy target for predators, as they are weaker and slow to move away from danger. To survive when released, your animal must therefore be strong and healthy.

One of Australia's larger marsupial predators, the eastern quoll is an efficient hunter, preying on mammals, birds, reptiles, frogs and invertebrates. Quoll populations have declined since European settlement due to loss of suitable habitat and competition from introduced predators, especially foxes, cats and wild dogs.

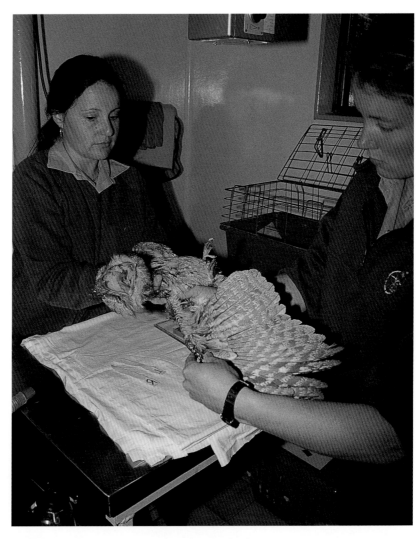

With multiple fractures of the right wing after a road accident, this tawny frogmouth will never regain complete wing movement. Frogmouths rely on quick, quiet flight to catch their prey, consisting mainly of ground-dwelling insects. Without the full use of both wings, this bird will have difficulty catching prey and will grow progressively weaker, making it more susceptible to disease and predation. It's often most humane to euthanase birds as severely injured as this one at the initial veterinary examination.

CHAPTER SEVEN
ETHICS OF WILDLIFE CARE

Some controversial issues relating to the principles of wildlife care.

Unfortunately it is not possible to save the life of every native animal that comes into care. In some instances it is more humane to end the life of an animal than to allow it to suffer further pain or hardship.

ORPHANED NEWBORN

This is best explained in the case of marsupial young, which are born in a very undeveloped state. During the early stages of pouch life they are blind and furless, with limbs and internal organs still developing. They also receive special antibodies from their mother's milk to help protect them from infection.

Research has shown that many of these immature young live for a period of time in captivity but just don't thrive. They are very susceptible to disease and eventually die. In this instance it is considered more humane to have them euthanased than to subject them to a life of suffering and hardship.

SEVERELY INJURED ANIMALS

Severe injuries, such as damaged joints, loss of limbs, loss of sight, broken beaks and permanent incoordination, will restrict an animal from behaving normally in the wild. If an animal is unable to catch or eat its food, it will eventually die. If it can't escape from predators it will also die. Under these circumstances it is more compassionate to euthanase it at the initial veterinary examination.

POOR QUALITY OF LIFE

If a native animal is incapable of being released after a reasonable period of time in care, it may be more humane to euthanase it than to keep it caged forever. This is especially important if the animal has already had a taste of freedom.

This applies to animals that are unable to accept confinement and their health is deteriorating, and those that do not fully recover from disease or an injury. It also applies to animals that have become so dependent on humans they could never live independently. If it seems highly unlikely that the animal will ever be able to fend for itself in the wild, the decision to euthanase must be considered.

CONTROLLING INTRODUCED SPECIES

Feral animals are domesticated species that were introduced into Australia and now live here as wild animals. Feral mammals include cats, pigs, horses, goats, camels, dogs, water buffalo and donkeys. Other introduced mammals include the rabbit, brown hare, deer, fox, house mouse and black and brown rats. Non-native birds include the house sparrow, common starling, spotted turtle-dove, laughing turtle-dove, feral pigeon, blackbird, mallard, common (or Indian) myna, spice finch, European goldfinch, greenfinch, tree sparrow, red-whiskered bulbul and the skylark.

As many of these animals have established themselves in such high numbers in Australia, wildlife carers may consider it their duty to euthanase introduced animals that come into care. In this way the carer plays a small role in supporting the native species that live in their local area, because introduced animals prey on native wildlife, demolish natural vegetation, spread exotic disease and compete with native animals for food and shelter.

Non-native predators such as foxes and cats can cause extinction of rare and endangered native animals and should never be released into the wild.

Just orphaned, this red-necked wallaby joey weighs a mere 26 g. Its eyes have not yet opened and its ears are still stuck to the top of its head. Unfortunately, furless joeys like this can't be saved. The kindest thing you can do is to humanely put them down.

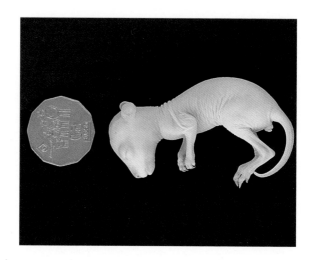

EUTHANASIA

Do not make the decision to euthanase a native animal by yourself – always seek a second opinion. Under normal circumstances you should contact your local vet, who will examine the animal thoroughly before deciding whether to euthanase. The most humane way to euthanase an animal is by an injection from your vet.

However, in extreme cases, where a vet can't be found and euthanasia is the only option, you may have to act promptly to alleviate the pain and suffering of an injured animal. Acceptable emergency options include using toxic car exhaust fumes, a sharp blow to an animal's head, wringing a bird's neck, driving over an animal's head or shooting. Cold-blooded animals such as reptiles and amphibians can be put into the freezer.

It is illegal for people to abuse or destroy native wildlife. However, in an emergency situation, it may be more compassionate to put an animal out of its misery as quickly as possible than to walk away and leave it suffering. Once the decision is made to euthanase, it is your duty to ensure it is done quickly and properly.

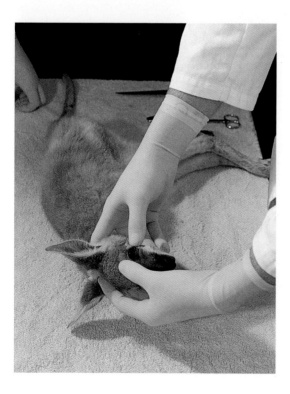

One of the hardest things for carers to accept is that many native animals die in captivity. Some are on their last legs when rescued and others just don't cope with the stress of being confined. Always consider having a post-mortem performed on the animal to determine the cause of death. The vet will learn more about wildlife by performing the examination, the carer will find out why the animal died and native animals benefit in the long run as more is learnt about them.

*Australia's largest raptor, the wedge-tailed eagle has a wingspan of up to 2.5 m.
Once persecuted, these birds are now fully protected as humans recognise their
contribution in controlling introduced pests such as rabbits. This hand-reared
orphan is around 14 months old. He is housed in a large aviary lined with smooth,
vertical wooden slats to prevent injury to his feathers, talons or beak.*

PART TWO

CHAPTER EIGHT
BIRDS

*Provides basic information on a variety of bird
groups and diets, together with feeding techniques
and housing for orphaned chicks.*

Australia has a wide variety of bird life and one of the many challenges for carers is to provide the right food for birds in captivity. They must take the time to identify each bird in their care so individual dietary requirements can be met.

A field guide to Australian birds will assist with identification. Take note of the length and shape of the bird's beak, the size and strength of its feet, the individual body shape and general colour markings. Even if you're unsure of the precise species, you should be able to slot the bird into one of the groups listed in this chapter, and therefore provide appropriate food.

A large proportion of natural food should be provided daily for the bird's health and wellbeing. Like many animals, birds eat a variety of food depending on the season. In spring and summer, pollen and insects are abundant and most birds with young to feed make the most of these high-protein food sources.

The supplementary food mixes outlined on the following pages are simple, and use basic ingredients. They are intended to be used only in the short term, and should be freshly prepared each day. The mixtures can be improved by adding a vitamin-mineral supplement (including calcium and phosphorus), using the dosage rate recommended by the manufacturer.

Commercial food products can also be used. These already contain the right balance of nutrients and when used in conjunction with the bird's natural food, they provide a well-balanced diet. For further information on these foods refer to the appendix (pages 144–6).

Clean drinking water must be provided every day for all species. The dish must be large enough to allow the bird to scoop water in its beak.

CARNIVORES

Carnivores are medium-
to-large birds with very
strong beaks that are usually
hooked at the tip. They include
kookaburras, butcherbirds and
magpies, as well as birds of prey
such as eagles, owls, falcons and
hawks. Birds of prey can be
dangerous to handle. They have
special needs and should be
handed over to a qualified carer as soon as possible.

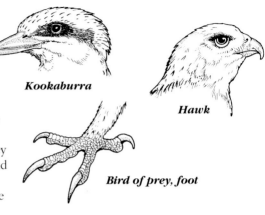

Kookaburra

Hawk

Bird of prey, foot

Carnivores eat whole animals and insects, including bones, fur, feathers and exoskeletons. Raw meat alone is not an adequate diet because it is deficient in calcium and other minerals and vitamins.

FEEDING TABLE FOR CARNIVORES	
Natural food:	• Mice and rats. • Lizards and small snakes. • Small birds and mammals. • Frogs and tadpoles. • Worms and centipedes. • Large insects – beetles, cockroaches, crickets, grasshoppers, stick insects, cicadas.
Supplementary food:	• Meatballs – moisten 50 grams of crushed dry dog food and mix with 100 g raw minced meat. Roll into Jaffa-sized balls. • Wombaroo Insectivore Rearing Mix.
Orphaned young:	• As above, using small or chopped food. • Pinkies (baby mice). • Whole dead animals such as mice can be filled with Wombaroo Insectivore Rearing Mix to provide extra nutrients.

Wisely using thick gloves in a specialised raptor-handling technique, this carer has separated the barking owl's legs, pointed its talons away from himself and secured its wings. Before seeking further assistance, carers can temporarily place raptors in a well-ventilated cardboard box in a cool, quiet place. Wire cages are unsuitable because excessive feather damage can occur.

Although captive tawny frogmouths will readily accept supplementary feeding, it's essential to also give them natural food. Before being released they must be able to recognise and catch their own food, such as ground-dwelling insects.

65

INSECTIVORES

Insectivores include small birds with pointed beaks such as magpie-larks, cuckoos, whipbirds, cuckoo-shrikes, swifts, drongos, dollarbirds, bee-eaters and pittas. Tiny birds such as robins, wrens, swallows, flycatchers and fantails are also included in this group.

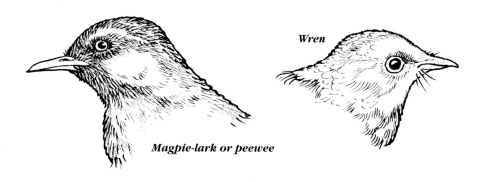

Wren

Magpie-lark or peewee

FEEDING TABLE FOR INSECTIVORES	
Natural food:	• Winged insects – mosquitoes, flies, moths. • Foliage insects – scale, aphids, bugs. • Ground-dwelling insects – beetles, ants, termites. • Spiders. • Caterpillars and worms. • Insect larvae.
Supplementary food:	• Insect crumble – mix until crumbly one mashed hard-boiled egg, a teaspoon of breadcrumbs and a tablespoon of crushed dry dog food. • Wombaroo Insectivore Rearing Mix. • Mealworms (use sparingly).
Orphaned young:	• As above, using small or chopped food. • Combine Wombaroo Insectivore Rearing Mix with water. Gradually progress to a drier mixture as the orphan develops.

Perched high in trees, sacred kingfishers search for large insects and worms on land, or tadpoles and small fish in shallow water. They dive to catch prey, taking it back to a branch where they bash it to death. In captivity they can be encouraged to eat by placing their food in a shallow water dish. In winter, sacred kingfishers usually migrate to northern Australia, New Guinea, Timor and the Solomon Islands.

67

Friarbird

Spinebill

Lorikeet

NECTIVORES

Nectivores are small birds with long, slender and slightly curved beaks. All possess a brush-tipped tongue which is used to extract nectar from flowers. They include honeyeaters, spinebills, wattlebirds, friarbirds, noisy miners, lorikeets and silvereyes.

FEEDING TABLE FOR NECTIVORES	
Natural food:	• Nectar and pollen from native flowers such as eucalypts, bottlebrushes and grevilleas. • Sap from wattles and eucalypts. • Manna, honeydew and lerp. • Soft fruits and berries. • Insects.
Supplementary food:	• Chopped, well-ripened fruit such as bananas, pears, pawpaws, grapes, melons and oranges. • Nectar mix – two tablespoons of high-protein baby cereal, one tablespoon of sugar and 100 mL water. • Wombaroo Lorikeet and Honeyeater Food.
Orphaned young:	• Add a mashed hard-boiled egg, mashed fruit and insects to the nectar mix. • Mix equal parts of Wombaroo Insectivore Rearing Mix and Wombaroo Lorikeet and Honeyeater Food.

Pet carry-cages provide safe, secure housing for orphaned fledglings like this little wattlebird (right). A variety of native blossoms such as bottlebrush, banksia and grevillea (below) should be offered to all nectivores daily to encourage natural foraging. Supplementary food is usually relished and provides the extra nutrients the birds need to stay healthy in captivity.

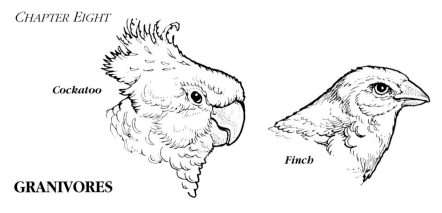

Cockatoo

Finch

GRANIVORES

Granivores vary dramatically in appearance, but generally have short, stout, conical beaks. They include finches, firetails and quails, some doves and pigeons, as well as parrots such as rosellas and corellas, galahs and cockatoos.

FEEDING TABLE FOR GRANIVORES	
Natural food:	• Seeds of native trees and shrubs such as eucalypts, wattles, casuarinas and banksias (offer branches with seed pods attached). • Grass seeds • Fallen seeds • Grain • Native fruit and berries.
Supplementary food:	• Commercial birdseed appropriate to species. • Chopped fruit and vegetables such as apples, pears, mangoes, corn cobs, lettuce and silver beet. • Soaked, sprouted seed – washed well. • Sand or shell grit should be available at all times to aid digestion and provide minerals.
Orphaned young:	• Use Roudybush Squab Handfeeding Formula (crop milk replacer) for feeding orphaned doves and pigeons from hatch to 1–2 weeks of age. • Fill crop at each feed, then feed again just before crop has completely emptied. • Egg food – mix a mashed hard-boiled egg with two tablespoons of high-protein baby cereal and a crushed Milk Arrowroot biscuit. Moisten with water. • Wombaroo Granivore Mix and Roudybush Formula 3 are complete foods for rearing orphans.

ANGELA SPENCER

In the wild, the king parrot (left) eats seeds, nuts, fruit and berries on a wide variety of trees and shrubs, as well as feeding on seeds on the ground. Granivores are often the easiest birds to care for due to their willingness to eat commercial birdseed. Of the various mixes available (below), choose one appropriate to the size of the bird in care. Use sunflower seed sparingly.

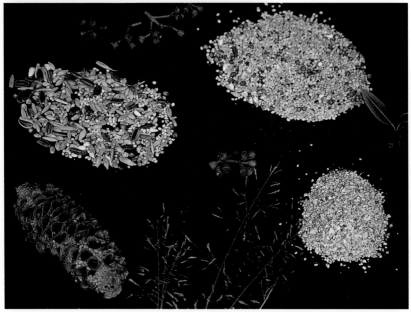

71

Fruit-dove

Catbird

FRUGIVORES

These are medium-sized birds with solid, deep beaks. They include bowerbirds, catbirds, figbirds, orioles and fruit-doves.

FEEDING TABLE FOR FRUGIVORES	
Natural food:	• Native fruit and berries. • Insects.
Supplementary food:	• Chopped, well-ripened fruit such as cherries, mulberries, guavas, figs, grapes and bananas. • Soaked dried fruit such as sultanas and raisins. • Wombaroo Insectivore Rearing Mix.
Orphaned young:	• Fruit balls – mix a mashed hard-boiled egg with a crushed Milk Arrowroot biscuit and two table-spoons of mashed fruit. Moisten with water and roll into small balls. • Add Wombaroo Insectivore Rearing Mix to puréed or mashed fruit.

Like most frugivores, satin bowerbirds live in rainforest and nearby eucalypt forest. Their natural diet is mostly fruit and berries, supplemented in season by insects and plant matter. When first feeding them, choose a fruit similar in shape and colour to their natural food.

WATERFOWL

Waterfowl are grass and insect eaters, and include swans, geese and a variety of ducks. They have broad, flat and blunt beaks, short legs and webbed feet.

Coots, moorhens and swamphens also fall into this category. These birds have a shield above their solid beaks and their feet are not webbed.

Sand or shell grit should be available at all times to aid digestion and provide minerals.

Coot

Coot foot

Duck

Swan

Webbed foot

Reared from tiny, downy ducklings, these Pacific black ducks are now ready to be released. Ducks can be set free when fully feathered, able to fly and properly waterproof. Always release them in a habitat where others of the same species are living.

73

As waterfowl are basically herbivores, their captive diet should be mostly plant-based and include a variety of grasses and grass seeds, berries, lettuce and grain. All waterfowl species need chicken crumble or pellets and shell grit for extra nutrients. Insects, snails, worms and other invertebrates are also eaten in the wild and should be provided to captive birds whenever possible.

FEEDING TABLE FOR WATERFOWL

Natural food:	• Grasses and herbs. • Aquatic vegetation. • Seeds from grasses and sedges. • Fallen berries. • Aquatic insects, particularly for diving ducks as they are highly insectivorous.
Supplementary food:	• Greens such as chopped lettuce, spinach, sprouts, clover, duckweed and grass. • Soaked, sprouted seeds – washed well. • Crushed mixed grain soaked in water. • Chicken pellets (use sparingly).
Orphaned young:	• Mostly finely chopped greens (as above). • Small portions of chicken crumble (available from pet shops and produce stores). • See precocial chicks (page 81).

Emus are also grazers, feeding mostly on grasses, seeds, berries and insects. As their diet is similar to waterfowl's, emus can be fed the same supplementary foods. They should have access to fresh water in a large, deep trough as well as coarse grit or fine gravel.

WADERS

These are medium-to-large birds with long, thin legs and toes and very long beaks. They include herons, egrets, ibises, spoonbills, brolgas, sandpipers, stilts, curlews and plovers.

Waders eat insects and whole fish – including scales, bones, exoskeletons, etc. They may need to be force-fed at first (page 78).

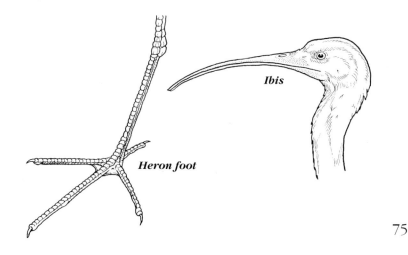

Ibis

Heron foot

75

Long-legged waders should only be housed where there's room for them to stand up. Permanent damage may result from forcing them to sit with legs bent. When handling, be cautious of the pointed beak – sunglasses may help protect your eyes.

FEEDING TABLE FOR WADERS	
Natural food:	• Aquatic insects. • Small fish, frogs and tadpoles. • Worms, snails and crustaceans. • Insects – beetles, grasshoppers, crickets.
Supplementary food:	• Pellets – mix together 100 g raw minced meat or fish and 50 g crushed dry dog food. Moisten with water and roll into long pellets. • Wombaroo Insectivore Rearing Mix.
Orphaned young:	• As above, using small or chopped food.

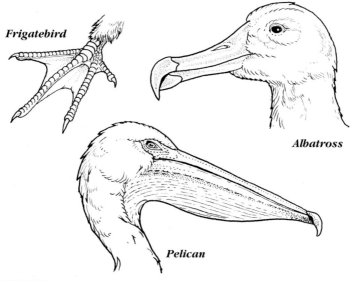

Frigatebird

Albatross

Pelican

SEABIRDS

Seabirds are medium-to-large birds with short legs, webbed feet and long, solid beaks which are usually hooked. They include penguins, albatrosses, shearwaters, petrels, cormorants, pelicans, seagulls and terns.

Seabirds fed solely on thawed frozen fish need extra vitamins such as Vetafarm Seabird Vitamin Tablets. Don't feed them tinned fish such as sardines or cat food.

FEEDING TABLE FOR SEABIRDS	
Natural food:	• Fish, squid, cuttlefish and crustaceans. • Fresh sea water daily.
Supplementary food:	• Whole fish such as whitebait, pilchards, yellowtail and red-spot whiting. Match the size of the fish to the bird's beak and feed them to the birds headfirst. • May need to be force-fed at first (pages 78 and 83). • Wombaroo Insectivore Rearing Mix can be stuffed inside fish to provide extra nutrients.
Orphaned young:	• As above, using small fish.

FEEDING TIPS

The Wombaroo Bird Food booklet (page 145) includes a guide showing how much food birds require every day. Generally, adult birds should be offered 10–30 per cent of their body weight in food each day.

A range of feeding methods can be implemented:

• **Crop feed** – insert a fine tube ("crop needle") into the crop or oesophagus to feed fluids to very weak birds. Always seek help from an experienced carer.

• **Dropper feed** – use a dropper to gradually feed a slurry mixture to very young birds.

• **Spoon-feed** – use a bent teaspoon to feed birds a thick fluid diet.

• **Tweezer feed** – narrow tweezers can be used to put solid food into a gaping beak.

• **Skewer feed** – skewer food on a blunt toothpick or twig and carefully place it at the back of the bird's mouth. Food can be first dipped in water to aid digestion.

• **Force-feed** – hold the beak open and place solid food at the back of the bird's mouth. Close the beak and gently stroke the neck to encourage the bird to swallow.

• **Fluid should never be poured into a bird's mouth.**

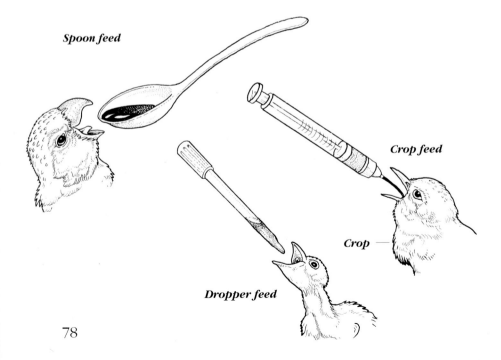

Spoon feed

Crop feed

Crop —

Dropper feed

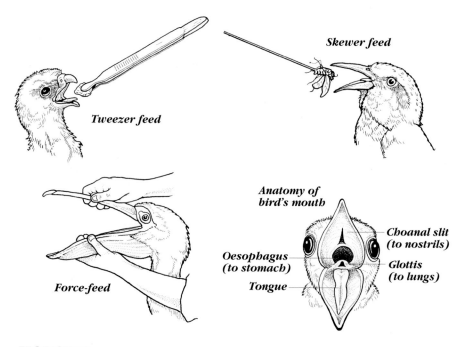

Tweezer feed

Skewer feed

Force-feed

Anatomy of bird's mouth

Oesophagus (to stomach)

Tongue

Choanal slit (to nostrils)

Glottis (to lungs)

HOUSING

Cardboard boxes are suitable for the first 24 hours of care, providing a dark place to help the bird recover, and the smooth sides help prevent feather damage. Choose a box to suit the size of bird, line it with a folded towel and puncture ventilation holes in the sides. The box should be placed in a warm environment.

Pet carry-cages are ideal for birds needing constant treatment as it is easy to recapture the bird. Secure a firm perch inside, cover the cage with a dark towel and keep it in a safe, quiet place.

Larger cages are suitable for orphaned birds and recuperating adults. Use tree branches for perches and try to provide a natural environment.

Aviaries for rehabilitation should be as large as possible to enable birds to build up flight muscles. Provide a covered area for protection from the elements and plant with native flowering shrubs. Place other natural vegetation inside for shelter and use tree branches of varying thicknesses for perches. A bird bath will encourage birds to preen, but a separate water dish should be placed in the shade and kept free of contamination.

Waterfowl, waders and seabirds need a large aviary set on grass. It should include a pond with rocks and logs at one end to allow the bird to rest near the water's edge. Pond water should be changed regularly.

Large birds such as sulphur-crested cockatoos need to be housed in large, solid cages made from heavy-duty wire mesh. Put the cage in a natural setting where the animal can see other birds. Ideally the cage should receive sunlight and have a covered area for protection from bad weather. Thick branches make good perches for parrots.

Waterfowl housing should be placed directly on the ground, allowing the birds access to grass and soil. It should have a covered area and be portable so that fresh pasture is always available. Provide a shallow water dish for drinking and a larger bath for paddling. Food dishes need to be removed and cleaned thoroughly at least twice a day.

REARING TIPS

Baby birds can be divided into two groups according to their stage of development at hatching:

Precocial chicks (e.g. the young of ducks, geese, plovers and emus) are covered in down and wispy feathers, can feed themselves and are able to move around independently.

These chicks should be housed in a waterproof box or large fish tank with a heat source at one end so they can approach or move away from the warmth. Temperature inside should be gradually decreased from 36°C (just hatched) to normal air temperature (fledgling).

Housing must be hosed out regularly throughout the day. It is preferable to have two boxes so one can be cleaned while the other is in use.

Food should be placed in a sturdy, flat dish. Replace with fresh food at regular intervals throughout the day. Water should be put in a solid, shallow dish that is partially filled with pebbles so the chicks stay dry.

Altricial chicks (e.g. magpies, swallows, honeyeaters, parrots) are born with no feathers and eyes closed. They can't feed themselves and are totally dependent on the parents for warmth, food and shelter.

Carers need to make a substitute nest for these chicks. Line a small container with dry grass or fine twigs and place in a warm environment. Gradually decrease the temperature from 36°C (just hatched) to air temperature (fledgling). Monitor this carefully – altricial chicks cannot move away from the heat source.

This 1 sq. m fish tank provides the perfect set-up for housing precocial chicks. A feather duster makes a good "mother hen", providing them with a soft place to hide. Towelling would make better bedding than straw, but in either case it should be changed frequently. Ensure the heat source does not create a fire risk.

A wooden box with an open-mesh lid for ventilation and a light globe for warmth makes a cosy home for altricial chicks. As these chicks can't move away from the heat, a thermometer is essential.

Orphaned altricial chicks must be fed often and at regular intervals during daylight hours. Warm the food once, feed and then discard leftovers. Water should be mixed with the food, the mixture becoming drier as the orphan develops.

Regardless of the type of chick, good **management skills** are needed. When handfeeding, take care not to spill any food on the bird's feathers and wipe its beak after feeding to remove any spilt food.

All new arrivals should be isolated. Sterilise all feeding utensils and wash your hands before and after handling each bird. Keep the housing clean, removing droppings after every feed.

Feather dusters make ideal "mother hens" – chicks can huddle together under the duster where they will feel safe and secure.

To prevent orphans from becoming too used to humans, cover your hand while feeding. Some carers have successfully used hand-puppets to prevent imprinting. Encourage natural foraging and disguise food dishes as much as possible. Also try to mimic the parent's bird call.

Young should be gradually weaned onto an adult diet. Weigh orphans daily to monitor their growth. Seek help if you have any problems. Any bird that appears fluffed up may not be well.

Aim to rear and release a few of the same species together, but ensure they are used to eating a natural diet before release.

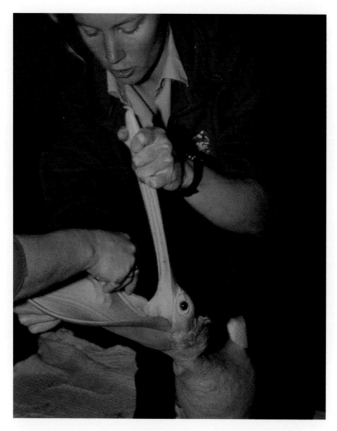

Two people are usually needed to force-feed a pelican. One secures the body and holds the beak open while the other dips fresh fish such as whiting in water and then places it headfirst down the bird's throat. The beak should then be closed and the throat gently stroked to encourage the bird to swallow.

FURTHER READING

Henderson, N. *Australian Bird Rehabilitation Manual.* Norma Henderson, Church Point, NSW, 1997.

Peters, C.A. *First Aid and Formulae for Feeding Sick, Injured and Baby Birds.* Bird Care and Conservation Society Inc., Adelaide, 1992.

Reader's Digest Complete Book of Australian Birds. Reader's Digest, NSW, 1986.

Brushtail possums are hardy and relatively simple to care for. New carers can gain valuable experience rearing an orphaned brushtail. Although known to eat a variety of food, these possums will be healthier and happier in captivity if provided with plenty of natural food – lots of leaf matter as well as native flowers, such as grevillea (above) and fruits.

Differences in size, colour and tail markings between the brushtail possum and the smaller ringtail possum are obvious when the animals are viewed together (opposite). Their habitats may overlap in the wild, but brushtails generally use the lower part of the tree while ringtails prefer the dense canopy, which provides the most protection from predators.

CHAPTER NINE
POSSUMS AND GLIDERS

*Covers the care and management of possums and
gliders, and includes growth charts for orphaned
brushtails and ringtails.*

Possums and gliders are nocturnal marsupials. Almost all are arboreal and well
adapted to life among the trees. There are marked differences in size, features and
diet between the species. Carers therefore need to accurately identify their possum and become familiar with its natural diet.

Brushtails are large, bold and very adaptable. They are solitary creatures and
prefer to sleep in dark places such as tree hollows. They have large ears and a
bushy tail.

Ringtails are medium-sized, agile possums with small ears and a smooth,
tapered tail. They are much more secretive than brushtails and harder to keep in
captivity. They often build their own nest, or drey, of twigs and bark, and live in
small family groups.

Gliders are small possums such as sugar, squirrel and feathertail gliders that possess soft-furred skin folds between the front and back legs. When extended, these membranes allow them to glide. During the day, gliders sleep in leaf-lined dens inside tree hollows. They rely heavily on the availability of mature, old-growth forests for their survival. **Greater gliders** are the largest of this group.

Pygmy-possums are tiny, elusive possums that make their own nests from leaves and strips of bark, usually in hollow logs. Both pygmy-possums and small gliders may become torpid during cold weather when food is scarce.

Squirrel gliders (right) do best when rehabilitated and released in small family groups. Small wooden nest-boxes make ideal substitute dens as they can be moved, with the gliders inside, to the release site, providing a familiar place from which the animals can disperse.

Ringtails make their own dreys, or nests (below), from shredded bark, twigs and leaves.

JOHN HANGER

FEEDING TABLE FOR POSSUMS AND GLIDERS

TYPE	BRUSHTAILS	RINGTAILS	GREATER GLIDERS	OTHER GLIDERS	PYGMY-POSSUMS
NATURAL FOOD:	Mostly leaves (particularly eucalypt), as well as flowers, buds, fruit, berries, grasses, herbs, fungi and occasionally insects.	Leaves, especially from eucalypt and rainforest trees, as well as native flowers and fruit.	Only specific eucalypt leaves – very fussy eaters. The species of leaf eaten varies considerably in different areas.	Eucalypt sap and wattle gum. Arthropods – moths, beetles, caterpillars and spiders. Also nectar, pollen, manna, honeydew and lerp.	Nectar from native flowers such as banksias and bottle-brushes. Arthropods – moths, beetles, caterpillars and spiders. Also pollen, fruit, berries and seeds.
	Feed possums a minimum of three different types of leaf. Cut fresh branches each day and keep them in water.				
SUPPLEMENTARY FOOD:	Fruit – apples, pears, grapes, bananas, oranges, melons, stone fruit, figs. Vegetables – carrots, corn cobs, spinach. Nuts – peanuts, almonds, pine nuts (give sparingly). Fresh water daily.		Greater gliders rarely accept supplementary food.	For gliders and pygmy-possums, sprinkle Wombaroo High Protein Supplement over fruit.	
ORPHANED YOUNG:	Refer to each milk-formula product label for directions on preparation and correct quantities.				
	• Wombaroo Possum Milk Replacer:		<.8 for joeys with less than 80 per cent of pouch life complete. >.8 for joeys with more than 80 per cent of pouch life complete.		
OR	• Biolac Milk for Marsupials:		M 100-G for furless joeys M 100 for furred joeys		
OR	• Di-Vetelact Low Lactose Animal Formula				

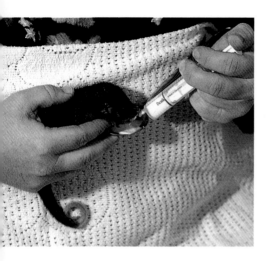

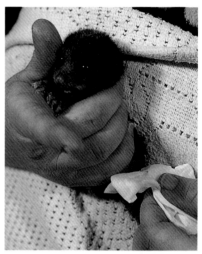

Tiny orphaned ringtails like this will often lap milk from the end of a syringe. They are easily stressed and should always go to an experienced carer.

Orphaned possums should only be "toileted" outside their artificial pouch once they are used to their carer.

FEEDING TIPS FOR ORPHANS

Possum teats are manufactured by Biolac and Wombaroo (pages 144 and 146). Before use, the carer must make a small hole at the end of the teat. This is best achieved with a thick, heated sewing needle. A 10 mL glass syringe or small bottle with a possum teat over the end can be used to feed young joeys. The best way to feed very tiny orphans is using an eye-dropper with a fine feeding tube attached.

Although possum joeys eat a small amount of solid food from a very early age, they rely heavily on the nutrients from their mothers' milk for growth and development. It is important, therefore, to choose a milk formula that contains the right balance of nutrients. Once the joey has accepted the new milk formula, encourage it to start lapping by pouring warm formula into a small dish that can't be toppled over. Most possum joeys will learn to lap very quickly.

Gradually introduce solid food, such as native blossoms and leaf tips, into the joey's pouch. Sweet, juicy fruit such as grapes and watermelon are also readily accepted. Possums eating solid food should excrete dark, firm pellets. Diarrhoea is unusual and should be investigated promptly.

REARING TIPS

The inside of a mother's pouch is warm and moist. This humid environment keeps the joey's skin soft and supple. Orphaned young have to adjust to drier pouches and drier heat, so it's essential to regularly lubricate the skin of furless joeys with a moisturising lotion. Sorbolene cream is light and absorbent, fragrance-free and completely safe to use on tiny joeys. Pure sorbolene cream (without glycerine or vitamin E) is available from most chemists.

Pouch-bound joeys need to be encouraged to excrete after every feed. This process is often called "toileting". Gently rubbing the vent with a moist cotton ball or soft tissue will usually cause the joey to start excreting.

Soiled joeys must be washed, dried thoroughly and placed in a clean pouch.

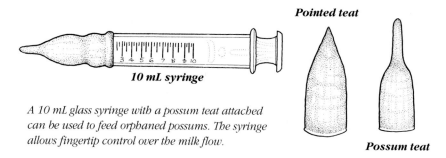

Pointed teat

10 mL syringe

A 10 mL glass syringe with a possum teat attached can be used to feed orphaned possums. The syringe allows fingertip control over the milk flow.

Possum teat

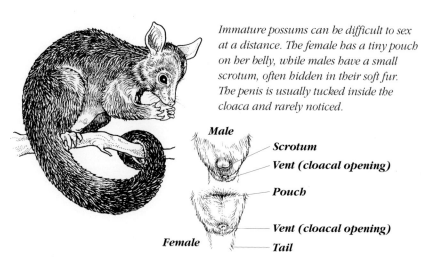

Immature possums can be difficult to sex at a distance. The female has a tiny pouch on her belly, while males have a small scrotum, often hidden in their soft fur. The penis is usually tucked inside the cloaca and rarely noticed.

Male

Scrotum

Vent (cloacal opening)

Pouch

Vent (cloacal opening)

Female

Tail

89

GROWTH CHART FOR ORPHANED RINGTAILS

WEIGHT	AGE	FEATURES	FOOD	HOUSING
(approx.) 45 g	2.5 months	Furless, eyes closed. Custard faeces.	Milk given 3-hourly around the clock, using eye-dropper and feeding tube.	Pouch, pet carry-cage, constant warmth 32°C; only for dedicated carers.
60 g	3 months	Just furred, eyes open. Thick custard faeces.	Milk – 5–6 feeds a day using syringe and possum teat; introduce solids to pouch.	Pouch, pet carry-cage, constant warmth 30°C; may start to explore cage.
80 g	3.5 months	Fine, sleek fur. Toothpaste faeces.	Milk – four feeds a day, may lap; put new tips, blossoms and fruit inside cage.	Pouch, pet carry-cage, constant warmth 28°C; confidently explores cage.
100 g	4 months	Short, fluffy fur. Soft pellets.	Milk – three feeds a day, lapping; eating leaves, flowers and supplements.	Cocky cage with wooden box high inside; place pouch inside box for security.
175 g	5 months	Thick fur. Dark pellets.	Milk – two feeds a day and decreasing; prepare to wean and increase solid food.	Cocky cage (keep outside), take pouch away; very active at night.
300 g	6 months	Fully independent.	Weaned; provide a variety of natural and supplementary food.	Large aviary; reduce human contact.
450 g	7 months	Prepare for release.	Decrease supplements, increase native food.	Large aviary; no human contact with possum.
600 g	8 months	Best time to release.	Offer only native food from release site.	Time to say goodbye.

NOTE: Ringtails are social animals and do much better when reared in small groups.

GROWTH CHART FOR ORPHANED BRUSHTAILS

WEIGHT (approx.)	AGE	FEATURES	FOOD	HOUSING
60 g	3 months	Furless, eyes closed. Custard faeces.	Milk given 3-hourly around the clock, using eye-dropper and feeding tube.	Pouch, pet carry-cage, constant warmth 32°C; only for dedicated carers.
100 g	3.5 months	Just furred, eyes open. Thick custard faeces.	Milk – six feeds a day using syringe and possum teat; introduce solids to pouch.	Pouch, pet carry-cage, constant warmth 30°C; hang pouch inside basket.
150 g	4 months	Fine, sleek fur. Toothpaste faeces.	Milk – five feeds a day. Add new tips, blossoms and grapes to pouch.	Pouch, pet carry-cage, constant warmth 28°C; may start to explore cage.
250 g	4.5 months	Short, fluffy fur. Soft pellets.	Milk – four feeds a day, may lap; put new tips, blossoms and fruit inside cage.	Cocky cage, attach wooden box up high; place pouch inside box for security.
400 g	5 months	Thick fur. Dark pellets.	Milk – three feeds a day, lapping; eating leaves, flowers and supplements.	Cocky cage (keep outside), take pouch away; very active at night.
650 g	6 months	Would still cling to mother's back in the wild.	Milk – two feeds a day and decreasing; prepare to wean and increase solid food.	Cocky cage outside; confidently explores cage at night.
900 g	7 months	Fully independent.	Weaned; provide a variety of natural and supplementary food.	Large aviary; reduce human contact.
1.2 kg	8 months	Prepare for release.	Decrease supplements, increase native food.	Large aviary; no human contact with possum.
1.5 kg	9 months	Best time to release.	Offer only native food from release site.	Time to say goodbye.

NOTE: Carers should aim to release orphaned possums when they are about half the average adult weight.

Housing for possums must be large enough for them to exercise properly. Leafy branches from eucalypts, wattles and banksias provide plenty of natural food and shelter. A deep wooden box secured high off the ground in a sheltered position is a necessity. Always provide extra boxes if you are housing a few of the same species together.

Large fine-wired cages are perfect for housing small gliders and pygmy-possums. This one is tucked away in a secluded part of a garden where the captive animals can watch the local wildlife feeding in the flowering shrubs nearby. This set-up will only work successfully if the housing is placed in an environment well away from domestic dogs and cats.

Small containers of sweet, juicy fruits placed well above the ground will supplement the natural diet of sugar gliders. Being highly insectivorous, these gliders will meticulously search fresh foliage, pouncing on spiders and caterpillars.

HOUSING

Pouches, essential for joeys, consist of an inner and outer layer. The inner pouch should be soft and flexible and made from natural fabric such as cotton. The outer bag should be heavier and warmer. Woollen or thick, fleece-lined bags are ideal.

An **electric heat pad** is the best way of providing constant warmth to orphaned possums. Use a thermometer to monitor the surrounding air temperature – 32°C for furless joeys, 28°C if they are furred. Once warmed, joeys can become very active, so make sure the heat source is on the outside of the cage.

Pet carry-cages provide safe, secure housing for orphaned joeys, small possums and injured adults. Place a towel at the cage's base and hang the pouch to one side. Cover the cage with a dark towel and keep it inside in a safe, quiet place.

Cockatoo cages are more suitable for larger joeys and convalescing adults. Again, a folded towel should be placed at the cage's base. Secure a wooden nest-box high in the cage and provide branches for climbing. Attach a sturdy bottle to one side to hold vegetation. Cover part of the cage with a dark towel.

Large aviaries are best for juvenile and adult possums, particularly if housing a few of the same species together. Situate the aviary in natural surroundings and secure wooden boxes, dreys and hollow logs high in the cage. Grow native shrubs inside and attach long water containers to hold other native vegetation. Include firm branches and rope for climbing, and a secure feeding tray in a sheltered position. Aviaries set up like this can also be used for self-release (page 55).

FURTHER READING

Smith, B. *Caring for Possums*. Kangaroo Press, Kenthurst, NSW, 1995.
Stanvic, S. *Possums*. Blue Mountains WIRES, Lawson, NSW, 1992.

PHOTOS: ROSEMARY BOOTH

CHAPTER TEN
KANGAROOS AND WALLABIES

Outlines the rehabilitation procedures for macropods and includes information on common diseases in captive joeys.

Kangaroos and wallabies are macropods. This term refers to the large group of terrestrial marsupials that have strong, powerful back limbs that enable them to hop at great speed.

Kangaroos and **wallaroos** are large macropods that live in dry, open grasslands and woodlands. They eat large quantities of coarse grasses such as kangaroo and tussock grasses.

Wallabies are medium-sized macropods that live in open grasslands and woodlands, with dense scrub for daytime shelter nearby. In the wild they eat short, green grasses, as well as shrubs and herbs.

Pademelons are small macropods that live in dense rainforests and moist eucalypt forests. They eat succulent green grass, grass seeds, shrubs and ferns, fallen leaves, fruit and berries, and fungi.

Bettongs and **potoroos** are very small macropods that generally build their own nests in thick tussock grass or dense scrub. Being so small, they require a more nutrient-rich diet such as fallen seeds and berries, grass roots, plant tubers, fungi and insects.

Around 2 kg in weight, the long-footed potoroo (opposite above) is losing habitat and often becomes a tasty meal for introduced predators. It is now an endangered species. The knowledge that wildlife carers gain from rehabilitating common species can be used to effectively manage captive colonies of endangered species such as this.

Differences between a male and female macropod are apparent when they are viewed together (opposite). The male red-necked wallaby, right, is larger, having well-developed muscles and a scrotum. The female is smaller and has a bulging pouch, indicating a joey's presence. The stain on her belly marks the pouch opening.

FEEDING TABLE FOR MACROPODS	
Natural food:	Native grasses. Pasture grasses. Seeding grasses. Grass roots and dirt. Bark on branches. Green leafy branches. Fallen leaves. Native fruit and berries. Fresh water daily.
Supplementary food:	Lucerne hay or chaff. Kangaroo pellets or goat pellets. Root vegetables such as carrots, parsnips and sweet potatoes.
Orphaned young:	• Wombaroo Kangaroo Milk Replacer: <.4 for joeys with less than 40 per cent of pouch life complete. .4 for joeys with 40 per cent of pouch life complete. .6 for joeys with 60 per cent of pouch life complete. >.7 for joeys with more than 70 per cent of pouch life complete.
OR	• Biolac Milk for Marsupials: M100 – early lactation milk. M150 – mid-lactation milk. M200 – late-lactation milk.
OR	• Di-Vetelact Low Lactose Animal Formula.

FEEDING TIPS FOR ORPHANED JOEYS

Macropod teats and feeding bottles are available from Biolac and Wombaroo (pages 144 and 146). The teats come in different sizes to suit the type of macropod and the stage of development.

Before use, the carer must cut a tiny hole in the end of the teat with a sharp pair of scissors. A needle-hole is too small for macropods.

Tiny joeys depend entirely on the nutrients in their mothers' milk for growth and development. This milk changes in composition throughout lactation to meet the joeys' special needs, so a milk formula must contain the right balance of nutrients and imitate the changes that occur naturally in the mothers' milk.

Product labels provide directions on correct quantities and how to prepare the formula.

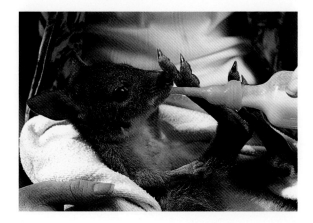

When first orphaned, joeys can be difficult to feed. They often feed better when their eyes are covered and their head gently held. This orphaned pademelon has adjusted to captivity and accepted a new milk formula.

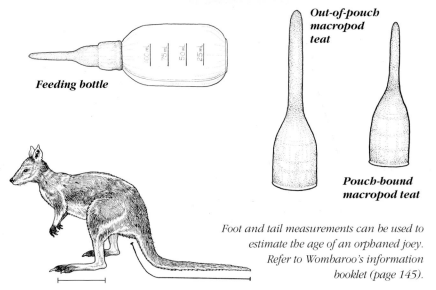

Feeding bottle

Out-of-pouch macropod teat

Pouch-bound macropod teat

Foot and tail measurements can be used to estimate the age of an orphaned joey. Refer to Wombaroo's information booklet (page 145).

Until a joey's stomach establishes special bacteria (called **gut flora**) that ferment plant matter, it will be unable to break down plant food adequately and absorb nutrients into the bloodstream. Once the bacteria are established, the faeces will become firmer and darker.

In the wild, a joey develops these important bacteria by nibbling on dirt and macropod faeces found among the grass where its mother is grazing. Orphaned joeys also need access to dry grass, grass roots and dirt from an early age. Always

97

When a female macropod is carrying young, her pouch becomes a warm and humid environment. She frequently licks the pouch lining to keep it clean and moist (right) and spends a considerable amount of time grooming her young.

Showing great interest in its mother's feeding habits, this seven-month-old joey imitates her foraging behaviour. The pouch hangs very low, allowing easy access to grass and soil. By this period of development – stage 4, page 103 – the joey's gut flora is well established.

gather dirt and grass from cat-free areas because of the risk of toxoplasmosis (page 109).

Gradually introduce food such as hay, grass and concentrates into the pouch of an orphaned joey. As it grows older, the food and water can be put in separate dishes and placed on the ground near the pouch.

It is important to record the joey's weight every week. The ideal growth rate reflects a growth pattern similar to that of mother-reared young. Generally, 5 per cent weight gain a week is poor, 10 per cent is good and 15 per cent is ideal. Under normal circumstances the percentage of weight gain per week slowly decreases as the joey's weight increases.

HOUSING

For **adult and juvenile macropods**, use a large, well-fenced grassy enclosure with natural shelter such as tussock grass, native shrubs and trees. A protected area inside the enclosure, such as an open garden shed with a concrete floor, will provide protection in bad weather and keep the feeding area clean and dry.

The enclosure should be well away from domestic dogs and cats. Make sure it contains no toxic plants, such as azaleas or oleanders. Avoid overcrowding and rotate or rest the enclosure periodically. All faeces should be removed daily.

Orphaned joeys need to be kept warm and snug in an artificial pouch. The bond that develops between the joey and its pouch can be very strong, like a child's with its security blanket. Pouches are used throughout a joey's development until it learns to sleep in a more natural way.

Low baskets (right) make ideal homes for orphaned macropods. It's preferable to line woollen bags because some joeys suck their pouches and loose fibres can be swallowed.

Sheets of metal around this well-fenced macropod enclosure (below) form a visual barrier against roaming dogs. The site is well drained, provides access to sun and shade and has plenty of native grasses.

Polystyrene boxes make ideal housing for furless joeys, especially in cold weather when it can be hard to maintain a constant 32°C without insulation. The digital thermometer on the left comes with a probe that is placed inside the pouch beside the joey to measure air temperature.

Furred joeys need to be kept inside a soft cotton pouch that is pinned to an outer bag and positioned so that the joey can hop out and in again unaided.

The outer bag should be tough and sturdy. Canvas haversacks are ideal and sheepskin bags are great in cold weather. Extra warmth can be provided by placing an electric heat pad underneath, or at the back of, the joey's outer bag.

The outer bag should be hung so that its base just reaches the ground. Alternatively, it can be placed inside a sturdy cane basket and kept on the ground.

Housing for **furless joeys** is slightly different. Place a well-wrapped heat pad or hot-water bottle in the base of a polystyrene box. Fill the box with a woollen blanket and make an opening in the middle to imitate a small pouch. Place the joey – wrapped in a soft, inner liner – deep within this makeshift pouch. A constant temperature of 32°C must be maintained and monitored closely.

REARING TIPS

For essential information on rearing joeys, see rearing tips, page 89.

ORPHANED-JOEY DEVELOPMENT

STAGE 1	
Appearance:	Furless, delicate pink skin; eyes closed, ears down.
Behaviour:	Pouch-bound, wriggles, unable to stand.
Warmth:	Constant 32°C.
Food:	Milk fed 2–3-hourly around the clock.
Faeces:	Yellow custard.
Skin care:	Apply lotion every 6 hours to whole body (page 89).
Special requirements:	Very hard to rear. Need specialist care, e.g. suitable humidity. Euthanasia recommended.

Extremely small and furless, **stage 1** *joeys have ears folded back against the head, unopened eyes and internal organs that are still developing. They are very difficult to rear and have a poor chance of survival.*

Much larger but still furless, **stage 2** *joeys have erect ears and their eyes are open. Their tender skin must be lubricated morning and night with sorbolene cream, to keep it soft and supple.*

101

*Approaching **stage 3** (above), this joey has fine silver fur coming through. By **stage 4** (right), all joeys have a good covering of short fur.*

STAGE 2

Appearance:	Furless, dark colour under skin; eyes open, ears up.
Behaviour:	Quite active in pouch, may try to stand in pouch.
Warmth:	Constant 32°C.
Food:	Milk given 4-hourly around the clock.
Faeces:	Thick yellow custard.
Skin care:	Apply lotion twice daily to whole body.
Special requirements:	Hard to rear successfully. Strict hygiene absolutely essential. Only for dedicated carers.

STAGE 3

Appearance:	Very fine covering of fur.
Behaviour:	Very active in pouch, can stand in pouch, starting to groom.
Warmth:	Constant 30°C, starting to maintain own body temperature.
Food:	Milk – five bottles a day, e.g. 6 a.m., 10 a.m., 2 p.m., 6 p.m., 10 p.m.
Faeces:	Mustard toothpaste.
Skin care:	Apply lotion daily to tail, feet and paws.
Special requirements:	Understand how to establish gut flora. Introduce solid food to pouch. Safe area inside to house joey.

Like this swamp wallaby (left), **stage 5** *joeys should take their bottles standing and graze for long periods, returning to their pouches only for security.*

Confident and independent, **stage 6** *juveniles (right) should graze all night and sleep on the ground during the day. Withdraw human contact.*

STAGE 4	
Appearance:	Short, sleek fur.
Behaviour:	Emerging from pouch, hops awkwardly near pouch.
Warmth:	28°C in cold weather and at night; able to maintain own body temperature.
Food:	Four bottles of milk a day plus solid food.
Faeces:	Olive green toothpaste, forming soft pellets.
Skin care:	Only if required to feet and paws.
Special requirements:	Solid food and water left near pouch. Position pouch so joey can hop out and in again unaided. Access to grassy area outside for short intervals.

103

STAGE 5	
Appearance:	Long, sleek fur.
Behaviour:	Gaining confidence out of pouch, becoming better coordinated, grazes near pouch.
Warmth:	Not required by day, 20–25°C at night.
Food:	Three bottles of milk daily, joey needs to graze outside.
Faeces:	Soft, dark green pellets.
Skin care:	Not required.
Special requirements:	Able to house joey outside all day in a well-fenced grassy enclosure. Joey's bedding to be kept outside in a protected area such as an open shed. Able to house a group of same species.

STAGE 6	
Appearance:	Dense, waterproof fur; toughened pads on feet.
Behaviour:	Confident out of pouch, well coordinated and agile, grazes day and night.
Warmth:	Not required.
Food:	Two bottles of milk a day and decreasing, prepare to wean; grass dominates the diet.
Faeces:	Firm pellets.
Skin care:	Not required.
Special requirements:	Able to house joey outside in well-fenced grassy enclosure day and night. Natural shelter available, e.g. shrubs. Reduce human contact.

STAGE 7 (pre-release)	
Appearance:	Good body condition overall, in excellent health.
Behaviour:	Sleeps during day under natural shelter; grazes late afternoon, night and early morning; prefers the company of other macropods to humans; darts quickly for cover when alarmed.
Food:	Natural food, decrease supplementary food.
Special requirements:	Aim to release in groups at the age when young in the wild would normally be independent of their mothers.

Native animals are rehabilitated so they can return to the wild, and ***stage 7*** *is the time to say goodbye. A number was tattooed on this wallaby's right ear to identify the animal if it came back into care.*

Once a joey reaches stage four of development, carers who don't have a well-fenced, safe, grassy enclosure should pass the animal on to a carer who does. There the joey should mix with a small group of its species. This will help it learn to forage for natural food and gain other survival skills that are necessary for its successful release back into the wild.

If you do pass your joey on to another carer, make sure that the pouches and bedding go with it. Let the new carer know what brand of milk you are using so that the joey can continue using the same formula at first. Once the joey has adjusted to its new home and new carer, then it can be encouraged to accept different housing or feeding arrangements.

COMMON DISEASES IN CAPTIVE JOEYS

It is essential for macropod carers to develop a solid understanding of the common diseases associated with the management of orphaned joeys. Carers should frequently assess their joey's health, minimise stress at all times and act quickly when problems arise. They should also evaluate and revise their own management skills and keep accurate and detailed records.

When assessing a joey, carers should take particular note of its progressive weight gain, appetite, body condition, body excretions and behavioural changes. A macropod's normal body temperature is 36°C (+/–1°).

STRESS is the underlying factor behind most diseases in orphaned joeys. It causes physiological changes within the joey, resulting in a weakened immune system, hormone imbalances and gastrointestinal disturbances. Symptoms include lethargy and depression, poor appetite, failure to thrive, declining body condition, diarrhoea, crying out, hair loss, flinching and body trembling, teeth grinding, and psychological symptoms such as anxiety, fear and frustration.

Stress can be caused by trauma due to accident or injury, changed living conditions, bad management by a carer and confinement.

CANDIDIASIS

Candidiasis, or thrush, is an infection caused by an increase of yeast organisms, *Candida* sp., which are always present in low numbers in faeces and in the environment.

Symptoms: Difficulty eating and swallowing.
Pea-soup-like diarrhoea with a bittersweet smell.
Inflamed or smelly mouth.
White, curd-like lesions in the mouth or vent.

Cause: Stress.
Poor hygiene and management.
Antibiotic use.
Sudden change in diet.
Very common in hand-reared joeys.

Treatment: Mycostatin or Nilstat (nystatin) oral drops.
Consult your vet for dosage rates.

COCCIDIOSIS

Coccidiosis is a parasitic infection caused by ingesting the parasite eggs (oocysts) that have been passed in the faeces of another infected animal. Oocysts can live for long periods in the environment, especially in damp conditions.

Symptoms: Diarrhoea (can be watery to dark and tar-like).
Severe gut pain (hunched stance).

Lethargy and weakness.
Sudden death.
Eastern grey kangaroos and whiptail wallabies
are very susceptible.

Cause: Moist, contaminated enclosures.
Poor hygiene and management.
Overcrowding.

Treatment: Consult your vet urgently for drugs such as Baycox
or Trivetrin.
Treat for dehydration (page 36).

Prevention: Remove faeces from enclosures daily.
Keep supplementary feed in clean dishes or racks
off the ground.

COLIBACILLOSIS

This is caused by infection of the gut with the bacterium *Escherichia coli*. It is very infectious.

Symptoms: Severe, unrelenting diarrhoea with bad odour.
Can have blood, white matter or mucus in diarrhoea.
General weakness.
Death.

Cause: Poor hygiene and management.

Treatment: Consult vet urgently for potent antibiotics.
Treat for dehydration.

DIARRHOEA (non-infectious)

Symptoms: Loose or watery faeces without blood, mucus or bad odour.
Dehydrated only, suffering no other symptoms.

Cause: Stress.
Sudden change in diet.
Gut flora imbalance.
Inappropriate diet – too much milk.
                  – irregular feeding times.
                  – formula prepared incorrectly.
                  – unsuitable milk product.

Treatment: Rectify the cause of the problem.
Give just Lectade or Vytrate for 12–24 hours to rest the gut
and rehydrate the animal.
Gradually introduce half-strength milk, increasing to full-
strength over 24 hours.
If diarrhoea persists, consult your vet.

MYOPATHY

Myopathy is a muscle disease caused by an electrolyte imbalance and a lactic acid build-up in muscle tissue.

Symptoms:	Increased heart rate.
	Muscle stiffness.
	General weakness.
	Dark urine.
	Death.
Cause:	Brought on by stress or unusual exertion (often after being chased or captured).
Treatment:	Consult vet immediately.
	Vitamin E selenium injection (e.g. Vitamin E Selen, made by Boehringer Ingelheim, dose 1 mL per 10 kg.)
	Fluid therapy to restore electrolyte balance and flush the kidneys.
	Check urine with a dipstick until pH and myoglobin return to normal (pH 6–8).
Prevention:	To reduce the risk of myopathy, Vitamin E Selen injection can be used before a stressful event, such as before juveniles are captured and transported to the release site.
	Keep joeys in a safe, dog-proof enclosure.

PNEUMONIA

A number of bacteria and viruses can cause pneumonia, but there is usually an underlying cause. Malnourished joeys are more likely to develop the disease, often with diarrhoea and septicaemia.

Symptoms:	Laboured or noisy breathing.
	Lethargy and depression.
	Poor appetite.
	Death occurs rapidly in severe cases.
Cause:	Chronic stress.
	Aspiration of milk or food.
	Inadequate warmth.
Treatment:	Consult your vet urgently for potent antibiotics.
	Treat for dehydration.

SALMONELLOSIS

This is caused by infection with the bacteria *Salmonella* sp., which are shed into the environment by infected animals. There is a high carrier rate in young and adult macropods. The bacteria are very infectious and can be transmitted to humans.

Symptoms: Severe diarrhoea (watery to black, tar-like or bloody faeces).

Severe depression, lethargy and weakness.

Infection, septicaemia and death can occur rapidly.

Cause: Stress associated with poor management.

Exposure to the bacteria.

Treatment: Consult your vet urgently for antibiotics.

Treat for dehydration.

TOXOPLASMOSIS

Toxoplasmosis is a parasitic infection caused by ingesting *Toxoplasma gondii* oocysts. Cats are the definitive hosts and the only species to pass the oocysts in their faeces. Oocysts can live for long periods in the environment, especially in moist soil.

Symptoms: Progressive weakness.

Unsteadiness.

Inability to drink properly.

Diarrhoea.

Loss of balance, head tilt and circling.

Death.

Cause: Access to contaminated feed or soil.

Treatment: Mostly unsuccessful – best to euthanase (page 61).

Prevention: Cats and macropods don't mix. All cats should be excluded from feed sheds and enclosures.

Be especially cautious of kittens and females with litters.

WORMS

Symptoms: Failure to thrive.

Diarrhoea.

Dull, lifeless coat.

Cause: Associated with captivity.

Overcrowding and contaminated enclosures.

Can be worse after wet weather.

Treatment: Take fresh faeces to your vet for examination.

Suitable drugs include Panacur 10, Systamex or Ivermectin.

Prevention: Remove faeces from the enclosure daily.

Rotate or rest each enclosure periodically.

FURTHER READING

George, H. *The Care and Handling of Orphaned Macropods*. Beaumont, NSW, 1988.

Grigg, G., J. Jarman and I. Hume (eds). *Kangaroos, Wallabies, Rat-Kangaroos*. Surrey Beatty, Chipping Norton, NSW, 1989.

109

JOHN HANGER

The grey-headed flying-fox feeds on a variety of flowering and fruiting trees, favouring eucalypts, angophoras, tea-trees, banksias and rainforest trees. Flying-foxes chew their food to a pulp, swallowing the juices, nectar, pollen and small seeds, then they spit out the pulp. Food passes quickly through their digestive system, the required nutrients being absorbed and the waste excreted in less than half an hour.

CHAPTER ELEVEN
BATS

*Details the differences between megabats and
microbats. Also includes information on the
Australian bat lyssavirus.*

Bats are nocturnal, placental mammals capable of sustained flight. They are
classified into two groups:

MEGABATS

Flying-foxes are large megabats that eat nectar, pollen and fruit from native trees.
Blossom-bats are small megabats that have a long brush-tipped tongue for gath-
ering nectar from native flowers.

Megabats use sight and smell to navigate and to find their food. They play a
major role within the environment, pollinating flowers and dispersing seeds from
native forest trees.

These bats have large eyes, big feet and no prominent tail. They have two
claws on each wing, on the thumb and first finger. Young are born furred and with
eyes open.

*Minor holes or tears in the wing
membrane are common in
rescued megabats. Don't have
them stitched as they will heal
naturally over time.*

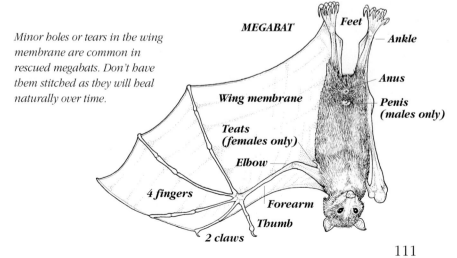

MEGABAT

Feet

Ankle

Anus

Wing membrane

Penis
(males only)

Teats
(females only)

Elbow

4 fingers

Forearm

Thumb

2 claws

111

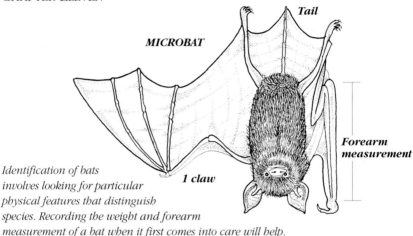

Identification of bats involves looking for particular physical features that distinguish species. Recording the weight and forearm measurement of a bat when it first comes into care will help.

MICROBATS

Microbats are tiny bats with small eyes and tiny feet. They have complex nose constructions, large ears, a prominent tail and one claw on each wing – on the thumb. Young are born furless and with eyes closed.

They feed on insects, using echo-location to navigate and find their food. As they can consume up to 50 per cent of their own weight in insects each night, they help to control insect populations. They hibernate in cold weather when insects are scarce.

Little broad-nosed bats weigh 8–12 g, have a broad, square muzzle and a tail attached to the tail membrane. They like to roost in small colonies inside tree hollows, emerging at dusk to feed on flying insects.

FEEDING TABLE FOR BATS

TYPE: MEGABATS

Natural food:	Flowers from native trees and shrubs such as eucalypts, paperbarks, banksias, bottlebrushes. Native rainforest fruits – figs, lilly pilly. Fresh water.
Supplementary food:	Chopped ripe fruit – apples, pears, grapes, melons, nectarines, mangoes, peaches and apricots. Wombaroo High Protein Supplement sprinkled over fruit.
Feeding tips:	Position food and water dishes level with their shoulders when hanging.
Orphaned young: **OR** **OR**	• Wombaroo Flying-fox Milk Replacer. • Di-Vetelact Low Lactose Animal Formula. • Nan 1 Baby Formula (available at chemists).

TYPE: MICROBATS

Natural food:	Mosquitoes, midges, flies, wasps, moths, beetles, bugs, weevils, cockroaches, ants, cicadas, crickets. Fresh water.
Supplementary food:	Mealworms coated with Wombaroo Small Carnivore Food.
Feeding tips:	Warm the bat in your hand before feeding. They may have to be handfed live insects at first.
Orphaned young:	• Wombaroo Insectivorous Bat Milk Replacer. Introduce solids gradually – first mealworm innards, then whole mealworms and insects.

DEVELOPMENT OF WILD GREY-HEADED AND BLACK FLYING-FOX YOUNG

AGE	WEIGHT	CHARACTERISTICS
BIRTH	*75 g	Fully furred with eyes open. Dependent on mother for warmth. Clings to mother's fur, suckles on a teat and is carried everywhere by her.
1 MONTH	*150 g	Able to maintain own body temperature. Still suckling from mother's teat. Left with other young bats at night while mother goes off to feed.
3 MONTHS	*300 g	Can fly. Able to eat natural foods. Starting to socialise with other bats of the same age in the colony.
6 MONTHS	*450 g (*approx.)	Completely weaned. Used to flying with the colony at night to forage for food.

DEVELOPMENT OF ORPHANED GREY-HEADED AND BLACK FLYING-FOX YOUNG

AGE	CARE AND FEEDING GUIDE
BIRTH	Provide constant warmth – 28°C (slightly higher for ill newborns or premature young). 5–6 bottle feeds per day.
4 WEEKS	4 bottle feeds per day. Allow bat to hang on portable clothes rack for short intervals.
5 WEEKS	No extra warmth required (for bats >150 g). Increased time spent on clothes rack.
7 WEEKS	Introduce solids (small pieces of steamed apple). On clothes rack all day.
8 WEEKS	Encourage to chew – introduce diced fruit. May start flying.
10 WEEKS	Reduce milk feeds, add milk powder to chopped fruit. On clothes rack day and night.
12 WEEKS	Feed chopped fruit sprinkled with milk powder at dusk. Provide native blossoms and fruit.
14 WEEKS	Bats to be placed together in one enclosure (creche).

REARING TIPS

Orphaned flying-foxes should be warmed and wrapped in a soft cloth before feeding, with their head lower than their feet. Use a flying-fox teat (available from Wombaroo, page 146) fitted over a 10 mL glass syringe or small glass bottle. Carers are encouraged to provide their orphan with a dummy. It will soothe the bat and also help prevent the animal biting the carer.

Bats must be kept clean and dry, particularly their wing membranes. Never cut their claws.

A plastic-coated clothes rack (below) makes an ideal frame for orphaned flying-foxes to practise hanging by their feet. A handtowel pegged to one end in the shape of a hammock will provide a soft, supportive area for the bat to rest. Ropes help larger flying-foxes move around their enclosure (right).

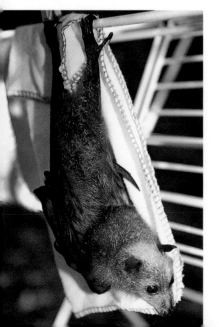

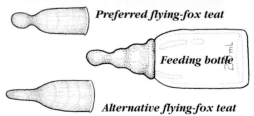

Preferred flying-fox teat

Feeding bottle

Alternative flying-fox teat

Orphans can be fed using a flying-fox teat attached to a small glass bottle or 10 mL glass syringe – the syringe allows fingertip control over the milk flow.

115

Cotton sacks tied to a rack can provide temporary housing for many microbats, with one or two of the same species being kept in each bag. A wooden box lined with cotton bedding and secured on top with a taut flyscreen lid makes a superb home for rehabilitating microbats.

HOUSING

A **pet carry-cage** can be used for tiny orphans needing constant warmth. Place a well-wrapped heating pad or hot-water bottle at the base and add plenty of bedding at a 45° angle. Cover the bat with soft cloth and hang with head lower than feet. Put a dark towel over the cage.

Monitor the temperature carefully, aiming for 28°C. Artificial heat may not be required in hot weather.

Larger cages (more than 75 square centimetres) made from small-wire mesh are suitable for juvenile flying-foxes and convalescing adults. The cage can be kept inside initially.

Aviaries are best for housing juvenile bats in a group so they can learn to socialise with each other and become less dependent on humans. Natural branches for roosting should be positioned high, and deep water containers used to hold native branches and blossoms.

Small wooden boxes or **fish tanks** with lids made of fine-wire mesh can be used for microbats. Secure cloth or bark to one end as a shelter and place the heat source outside the box at one end, taking care to provide gentle warmth only. Orphaned microbats require humid warmth, so put a moist sponge between the heat source and youngster.

LYSSAVIRUS IN BATS

Australian bat lyssavirus is currently known to infect both megabats and microbats. It's closely related to, though quite distinct from, the rabies virus.

Humans are at risk if an infected bat pierces the skin with a bite or scratch, allowing the virus to enter exposed tissue or nerve endings. Saliva and blood from an infected bat are also a risk if they contact broken skin.

Carers are urged to take precautions against infection. Hands should be washed thoroughly after handling each bat and carers should reduce the risk of being bitten or scratched by wearing thick gloves and long-sleeved shirts.

Many wildlife carers throughout Australia have rescued, rehabilitated and released thousands of native animals over many years without any detriment to their own or their families' health. However, in November 1996, a wildlife carer from Rockhampton in Queensland developed encephalitis and died after being exposed to this newly identified virus.

Until more is known about the Australian bat lyssavirus, bat carers are urged to adopt a responsible attitude to the following guidelines and to take proper precautions against infection.

Yellow-bellied sheathtail-bats weigh 30–60 g and have a pointed muzzle and a tail protruding from the tail membrane. Their belly colour can vary from yellow to white. At the time of writing, the Australian bat lyssavirus had been found in this species and four species of flying-fox.

ANGELA SPENCER

*To minimise the risk of infection with Australian bat
lyssavirus it is advisable to handle or restrain all flying-
foxes with long, heavy-duty gloves.*

Pre-exposure vaccination is recommended for people who wish to handle
bats. It consists of three subcutaneous or intramuscular injections of 1 mL rabies
vaccine. Contact your local doctor for further details.

Post-exposure vaccination is recommended for people who have been bitten or scratched by a bat within the last three months. It consists of five
subcutaneous or intramuscular injections of 1 mL rabies vaccine plus a single
injection of rabies immunoglobulin.

Rabies immunoglobulin, when required, should be administered at the same
time the first rabies vaccination is given. Contact your local doctor or health
department for further details.

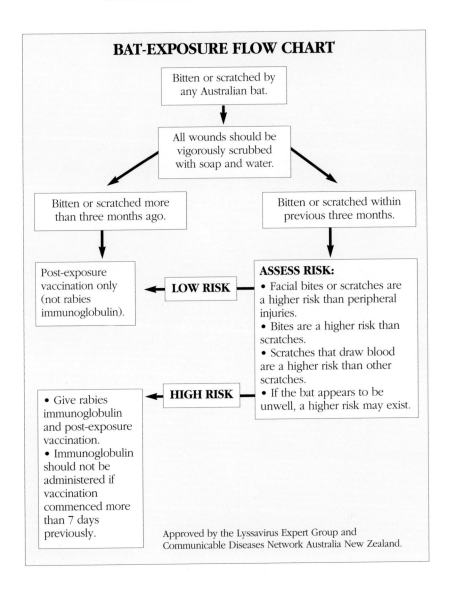

FURTHER READING

Collins, L. *Hand-rearing and Development of the Orphaned Flying-Fox.*
Linda Collins, Nimbin, NSW, 1995.

Nocturnal tree-dwelling colubrids, brown tree snakes feed mostly on small mammals and birds. Land-dwelling snakes in the colubrid group usually have solid teeth but no fangs or venom glands. Brown tree snakes differ, having rear fangs that eject venom, although the poison is not strong enough to seriously affect humans. They should be treated with caution nevertheless, as they can become very hostile when provoked.

CHAPTER TWELVE
REPTILES AND FROGS

*Covers the food and housing requirements for
lizards, land snakes, freshwater turtles and frogs.*

Reptiles and frogs are ectothermic – they rely on external heat sources to regulate their body temperature.

Both groups have special needs, so it is important to have a thorough knowledge of their specific requirements when caring for them. Some carers may have the facilities to rehabilitate smaller animals, but large monitors and snakes should always go to a herpetologist.

The reptiles that most commonly come into care are lizards, land snakes and freshwater turtles. These animals hibernate in cold weather.

In cool weather people often find reptiles that are sluggish and cold to the touch. When brought into care and provided with warmth they soon become active and look for food. Food should only be given to reptiles when constant warmth is maintained, as they need it to fully digest their food.

Some people have difficulty distinguishing between snakes and lizards. Lizards have legs (except legless lizards); solid, fleshy tongues (except goannas); external ear openings (most do); long tails (longer than snout to vent); and are non-venomous. Snakes, on the other hand, have no legs; deeply forked tongues; no ear openings, a short tail (shorter than snout to vent); and can be venomous.

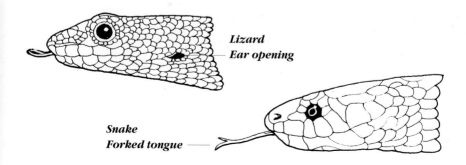

Lizard
Ear opening

Snake
Forked tongue

FEEDING TABLE FOR LIZARDS

TYPE	SKINKS	LEGLESS LIZARDS	GECKOS	DRAGONS	MONITORS
DESCRIPTION	Common, sun-loving lizards with smooth, shiny scales.	Snake-like lizards with no obvious legs.	Small, soft-skinned nocturnal lizards commonly found in warm environments.	Large lizards with well-developed limbs and dull, rough scales.	Large lizards with long, forked tongues and powerful claws. Great hunters and scavengers.
FOOD IN THE WILD	Insects, snails and worms. Larger skinks such as blue-tongues and shingle-backs also eat native fruits, berries and plants.	Spiders, insects and other small lizards.	Insects, spiders and even other geckos.	Insects, spiders, worms, small lizards, birds, mice and occasionally plants.	Insects, reptiles, birds, mammals and carrion.
FOOD IN CAPTIVITY	Insects – flies, moths, beetles, crickets, grasshoppers, cockroaches. Snails. Earthworms.	Fresh water daily (in a solid, shallow dish).		Dragons and monitors can also be fed mice, rats or day-old chicks. Many lizards, especially dragons, need to be sprayed with water daily to encourage lapping of droplets.	
SUPPLEMENTARY FOOD	As many large skinks are omnivorous, they should also be given green, leafy vegetables and chopped fruit.	Mealworms, crickets, cockroaches. Pinkies (baby mice). Wombaroo Reptile Supplement.			

Monitors, or goannas, can be aggressive, so it is advisable to hold the head and tail securely, with the claws facing away from the handler (left). Unlike some other lizards, monitors and dragons can't drop their tail to escape danger.

Geckos (right) differ from other lizards in having a fixed, transparent scale that protects the eye and is moistened and wiped clean with their wide, flat tongue. Some geckos also have adhesive pads on their toes.

JONATHON HANGER

FEEDING TIPS

Lizards do best on a varied diet of live food. Small lizards should be fed once a day and large lizards 3–4 times a week, although large monitors need only be fed once a week.

If lizards won't eat, beat a raw egg in a shallow dish and put the lizard's snout in the food – most will relish this special treat.

HOUSING

A wooden box with a tight-fitting fine-wire-mesh lid for ventilation and a perspex or glass front is ideal. Fish tanks with a similar lid are also suitable. The housing should be escape-proof, lined with newspaper and ideally exposed to sunlight for a short time each day.

It should include a nest-box, loose bark or leaf litter for shelter, and at one end, a basking platform (large rock) underneath a light globe. The temperature on the platform should be about 30°C.

All faeces, shed skin and uneaten food should be promptly removed.

123

SNAKES

All unidentified snakes must be regarded as potentially dangerous and should only be handled by experienced people.

FEEDING TABLE FOR SNAKES	
TYPE: **Description:** **Food in the wild:**	**BLIND SNAKES** Small, non-venomous, worm-like snakes. They have tiny, poorly developed eyes and live underground. Mostly ants, termites and pupae, as well as soft-bodied insects and worms.
TYPE: **Description:** **Food in the wild:**	**PYTHONS** Large, non-venomous snakes that use constriction to kill, suffocating their prey. Mammals, birds and reptiles.
TYPE: **Description:** **Food in the wild:**	**COLUBRIDS** Although rear-fanged snakes such as the brown tree snake are venomous, none are dangerous to humans. Mostly found in warm, moist environments. Predominantly frogs, tadpoles, small fish and lizards, as well as small birds, mammals and eggs.
TYPE: **Description:** **Food in the wild:**	**ELAPIDS** The most dominant group of land snakes in Australia. All are venomous, but only some are dangerous to humans. Although most prefer to retreat rather than attack humans, all will strike with their front fangs when threatened. Mammals, reptiles, frogs and birds.
Food in captivity: (except for blind snakes) **Supplementary food:**	Whole mice and rats. Day-old chicks. Fresh water daily. Wombaroo Reptile Supplement.

FEEDING TIPS

Most snakes in captivity can be fed whole mice, rats or day-old chicks about once a week. They usually require live food at first to stimulate feeding, but dead food is preferable, because live rodents may attack and injure the snake.

Snakes should be given fresh water daily in a solid, shallow dish.

124

Housing for pythons should be at least 1 m in height and include a branch for climbing and a wooden box to hide in. A light globe at one end should provide a temperature of around 25–30°C. Red or blue globes can be used at night to generate warmth with dim lighting.

Wriggling dead prey with forceps imitates live movement and encourages snakes to eat. Pythons will readily accept prey such as mice or rats, which can be purchased from pet shops. Frozen animals must be fully thawed before use. After feeding, snakes should be left undisturbed in a warm environment.

ANGELA SPENCER

HOUSING

Escape-proof housing is essential. Use a perspex- or glass-fronted wooden box or fish tank with a tight-fitting, fine-wire-mesh lid. Line the base of the box with newspaper and provide a wooden nest-box for shelter and a large rock for basking. A heat source at one end of the box should provide a temperature of 25–30°C.

All faeces, shed skin and uneaten food should be promptly removed.

125

FRESHWATER TURTLES

Living mainly in freshwater rivers and creeks, long- and short-necked turtles (often called tortoises) can also be found on dry land basking in the sun. To survive in captivity they need access to land and water.

FEEDING TABLE FOR TURTLES	
Food in the wild:	Aquatic animals such as crustaceans, tadpoles, snails, worms, small fish and insects.
Food in captivity:	Small fish, yabbies and prawns, earthworms, tadpoles, water snails and large insects.
Supplementary food:	Chopped mice, mealworms, Wombaroo Reptile Supplement and commercial pellets.

Large aquariums (below) make ideal housing for turtles such as this short-necked species (right). The platform on the left of the aquarium enables them to dry off and warm up under ultraviolet lighting, and aquatic plants, logs and rocks provide a natural setting.

FEEDING TIPS

Juveniles should be fed once a day, but adults need only be fed three times a week. The food should be chopped into bite-sized pieces and offered in water, but all uneaten food must be removed promptly from water to avoid contamination. Try to provide a high proportion of natural food.

HOUSING

Fill a fish tank sufficiently to allow the turtle to swim underwater comfortably. Replace the water daily and test its pH level – pH 7 is ideal and will reduce risk of disease.

Provide aquatic plants for shelter and an area of dry land inside the tank, such as a large, flat rock.

The tank should have access to sunlight for a short time each day and a heat source may be required, the ideal water temperature being 25°C.

FROGS

Frogs are amphibians that generally hibernate in cold or dry weather, becoming most active on warm, wet nights. They don't drink, obtaining most of their water requirements by absorption through their skin.

Most tree frogs have adhesive discs on the tips of their fingers and toes, making them superb climbers. Burrowing frogs live under the ground where they are protected from extreme weather conditions.

MIKE LANGFORD

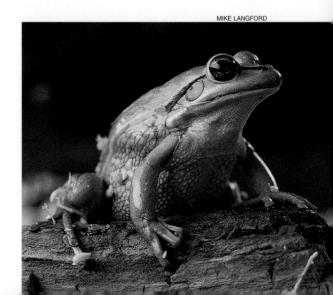

To identify a frog, study its colour, skin texture and features. Green and gold with a white belly, this large specimen has blue on the groin and thigh, granular skin, finger and toe discs, and webbing on the toes, confirming it as a green and golden bell frog.

Always release frogs back to the area where they were found – ideally on a warm, wet evening.

Carers in Queensland, the Northern Territory and northern New South Wales should be aware of the cane toad, introduced to Queensland in 1935 to help control sugarcane beetles. These toads breed prolifically, have few predators in Australia and many native mammals, birds and reptiles die after eating them. People are urged to actively destroy these pests. To kill a cane toad humanely, put it in a plastic bag, tie it securely and place it in the freezer. Wash your hands thoroughly after handling cane toads.

FEEDING TABLE FOR FROGS	
Natural food:	Insects such as flies, moths, slaters, beetles, bugs, cockroaches, crickets, grasshoppers, ants and termites. Spiders. Centipedes and caterpillars.
Supplementary food:	Mealworms and earthworms.

FEEDING TIPS

Frogs require live food – motion initiates feeding, but only offer food when constant warmth can be maintained. They do best when given a varied, natural diet.

HOUSING

Fish tanks with tight-fitting, fine-wire-mesh lids are best. Put loose soil or fine sand on the base and cover with leaf litter. Imitate the natural environment, with plants, loose bark and a hollow log. Sink a solid, shallow water dish into the soil.

Provide a heat source at one end of tank (an infra-red globe is best), but try to keep the temperature at 15–20°C. Use a water sprayer to keep housing moist, but only use tap-water that has been standing for at least 24 hours, rainwater or pond water.

Only keep similarly sized frogs together.

FURTHER READING

Cogger, H. *Reptiles and Amphibians of Australia*. Reed Books, Chatswood, NSW, 1996.
Weigel, J. *Care of Australian Reptiles in Captivity*. Reptile Keepers' Association, Gosford, NSW, 1988.

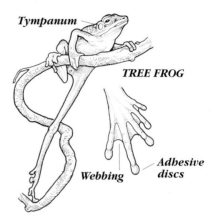

Tympanum

TREE FROG

Adhesive discs

Webbing

Housing for tree frogs should include a base of soil and leaf litter with plenty of branches and plants for cover (left). A light globe can provide gentle warmth and a shallow water dish is essential. Lightly spraying water in the enclosure (below) helps create a humid environment.

RANDY LARCOMBE

When threatened, echidnas (above) roll into a spiny ball or wedge themselves into the ground.

This baby echidna (right), about 70 days old, was fast asleep in a burrow when she was run over by a plough, resulting in amputation of her right leg. Born without spikes, echidna young are carried in the mother's pouch. When they're too big, they're left in a burrow while the mother searches for food.

ROSEMARY BOOTH

130

CHAPTER THIRTEEN
MISCELLANEOUS MAMMALS

Briefly discusses the care of echidnas, platypuses, koalas, wombats, bandicoots and native rodents.

Echidnas, platypuses, koalas, wombats, bandicoots and native rodents do not come into care as often as animals listed in previous chapters.

People finding echidnas, platypuses, koalas or wombats in distress should immediately contact their nearest wildlife authority because they have highly specialised needs. Their fate often depends on them receiving expert attention as soon as possible.

ECHIDNAS

These monotremes have prickly spines over much of their body and tough, spade-like claws.

They are sensitive to extreme weather conditions, hibernating in cold weather and avoiding the heat by foraging at night.

It is normal for echidnas to blow clear bubbles from their nostrils, which are situated at the end of a long, sensitive snout.

Echidnas feed on ants and termites, often ingesting a considerable amount of soil and nest material in the process.

Natural food:	Ants and termites. Fresh water daily (in deep, solid dish).
Supplementary food:	Mix Wombaroo Small Carnivore Food with water and soil from an ants' nest until food becomes moist and crumbly.
Orphaned young:	Wombaroo Echidna Milk Replacer. Multi-staged formulas available. Nestling echidnas only require milk once every 48 hours. Initially encourage young to suck milk from a cupped hand. Later they can be taught to drink from a solid dish.

HOUSING

A sheltered, outside enclosure is best. As echidnas can escape by burrowing, the floor should be lined with heavy-duty wire mesh below ground level and then covered with soil and leaf litter. Rotting logs (full of termites) and ant mounds can be placed on top. The soil and leaf litter must be replaced regularly.

Air temperature should be monitored and kept below 25°C.

Echidnas are good climbers – they can scale wire fences. The enclosure's sides should therefore be smooth and high.

FURTHER READING

Augee, M.L. and B. Gooden. *Echidnas of Australia and New Guinea.* University of NSW, Sydney, 1993.

George, H. *Echidnas – Rescue Rehabilitation Release.* Helen George, Beaumont, NSW, 1996.

PLATYPUSES

These monotremes live in freshwater lakes, streams and rivers. They have a leathery, duck-like bill, webbed feet and waterproof fur.

Platypuses feed underwater on insects, crustaceans, molluscs, worms, small fish and frogs. They also eat the larvae of caddis flies, beetles, mayflies and dragonflies. Their food is stored in cheek pouches until they surface, when they grind the food, spitting out the indigestible bits and swallowing the rest.

Most carers should only look after platypuses in emergency situations.

Natural food:	Yabbies and prawns. Earthworms. Insects.
Supplementary food:	Mealworms.

FEEDING TIPS

Put 15–30 cm of rain- or pond water in a bath. Provide a large rock or platform at one end and put the food in the water.

HOUSING

Use a smooth, wooden box and line the bottom with folded towels.

Platypuses are extremely sensitive to heat so keep the air temperature below 25°C.

KOALAS

Koalas are herbivorous marsupials well adapted to living in trees. They have strong limbs, razor-sharp claws and dense fur. The young are pouch-bound for seven months, then carried on their mother's backs for another five months.

Although wild koalas may look cute and cuddly, they can inflict nasty bites and scratches if handled incorrectly.

Koalas are specialised leaf-eaters, feeding at night almost exclusively on eucalypt leaves. They are very particular about their food, so it is imperative that the right species of eucalypt leaf is provided in captivity. The carer should have a thorough knowledge of koalas' preferred food-trees in their area.

Nearly ready to go back to the wild, this male koala (left) is on its way to be weighed, a weekly event in captivity. Koalas in care quickly adapt to routine management procedures such as this.

Captive koalas need a stress-free environment such as an aviary that provides protection from predators and bad weather, solid forked trees and fresh eucalypt leaves with plenty of new growth. Freshly cut branches must be kept in water containers and, in hot weather, frequently sprayed with water.

FEEDING TABLE FOR KOALAS

Natural food:	Queensland River red gum (*Eucalyptus camaldulensis*) Narrow-leaved red ironbark (*E. crebra*) Spotted gum (*E. maculata*) Grey gum (*E. propinqua*) Forest red gum (*E. tereticornis*)
	New South Wales River red gum (*E. camaldulensis*) Flooded gum (*E. grandis*) Tallowwood (*E. microcorys*) Grey gum (*E. punctata*) Sydney blue gum (*E. saligna*)
	Victoria and South Australia River red gum (*E. camaldulensis*) Tasmanian blue gum (*E. globulus*) South Australian blue gum (*E. leucoxylon*) Swamp gum (*E. ovata*) Manna gum (*E. viminalis*)
Supplementary food:	ProSobee Soy Infant Formula (available from chemists). The powder can be mixed with water to form a thick paste, then syringe-fed to debilitated koalas to provide them with extra nutrients. Fresh water daily.
Orphaned young: OR OR	• Wombaroo Koala Milk Replacer. Multi-staged formulae available • Di-Vetelact Low Lactose Animal Formula • Portagen Infant Milk Formula (available from chemists).

FEEDING TIPS

At least three different species of leaf should be fresh-cut each day. Branches should be at least 1 metre in length and covered in good tips.

HOUSING

In an aviary, place sturdy, forked tree branches for the koala to rest in. Deep water containers will hold freshly cut foliage.

The aviary should have access to sunlight and a covered area for shelter.

Faeces and fallen leaves should be removed daily.

FURTHER READING

Phillips, B. *Koalas – The Little Australians We'd All Hate to Lose.* AGPS Press, Canberra, ACT, 1990.

Phillips, K. *Koalas – Australia's Ancient Ones.* Macmillan, New York, USA.

WOMBATS

Wombats are large, solid, burrowing marsupials with short legs, powerful spade-like claws and coarse fur.

Wombats are herbivorous. They spend the day inside an underground burrow, emerging at night to feed on coarse native grasses, sedges, rushes, succulent plant roots and pasture grasses.

Wild adult wombats do not fare well in captivity. Every attempt should be made to return them to the wild within 36 hours.

Natural food:	Native grasses such as kangaroo and tussock grasses. Fresh water daily (in a large, solid dish).
Supplementary food:	Meadow hay or coarse lucerne.
Orphaned young: OR	Wombaroo Wombat Milk Replacer. Multi-stage formulas available Di-Vetelact Low Lactose Animal Formula.

HOUSING

Housing needs to be sturdy and escape-proof. The sides of an outside enclosure should be solid and high, and made of metal or wood (not wire). An old stable may suffice. Put a strong wooden box in one corner for shelter.

Ideally, wire mesh should cover the floor below ground level to prevent escape. The air temperature should be kept below 25°C.

FURTHER READING

George, H., G. Parker and P. Coote. *Common Wombats – Rescue Rehabilitation Release.* Helen George, Beaumont, NSW, 1995.

Triggs, B.E. *The Wombat – Common Wombats in Australia.* University of NSW, Sydney, 1996.

BANDICOOTS

These small, ground-dwelling marsupials have coarse, sleek fur and long, pointed snouts. During the day they sleep among dense vegetation and leaf litter, but at night they forage for insects, spiders and grubs, and fruit and plant roots and tubers.

Bandicoots are omnivores, feeding on or under the ground. Although seldom seen, they often leave deep conical holes in the lawn.

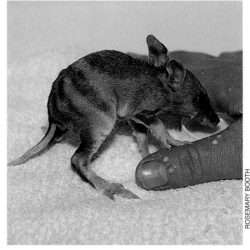

ROSEMARY BOOTH

Natural food:	Insects – beetles, cockroaches, crickets, grasshoppers, ants and termites. Insect larvae. Spiders. Earthworms and snails. Berries and seeds. Soft roots and tubers. Fresh water daily.
Supplementary food:	Mealworms. Dry dog food. Well-ripened chopped fruit. Wombaroo Small Carnivore Mix.
Orphaned young: OR	• Wombaroo >.7 Kangaroo Milk Replacer. • Di-Vetelact Low Lactose Animal Formula.

HOUSING

Bandicoots should be housed in an aviary with soil or leaf litter on the floor to encourage natural foraging. Also provide plenty of dense vegetation, long grass, hollow logs and clumps of compost.

Wire mesh should cover the floor well below ground level to prevent escape by bandicoot or entry by vermin. The aviary should have walls of solid metal or wood about 1.2 m high. The roof should be made of wire mesh, with covered shelter at one end.

All bandicoots will lap milk from an early age, like this 44-day-old eastern barred bandicoot (opposite). As this species is extremely rare on the mainland, injured or orphaned animals must go to experienced carers.

Orphaned bandicoots do best in enclosures with soil and leaf litter (right). Live insects can be tossed in to encourage them to catch their own prey.

DASYURIDS

Dasyurids are carnivorous marsupials such as the Tasmanian devil, quolls, antechinuses, phascogales, dunnarts and planigales. They are generally nocturnal.

In the wild they feed on small mammals, birds, reptiles, insects and carrion. Grasses, fruit and berries are also included in their diet at times.

Natural food:	Insects – beetles, bugs, cockroaches and crickets. Centipedes. Spiders. Rats and mice. Day-old chicks. Fresh water daily.
Supplementary food:	Pinkies (baby mice). Dry dog food. Mealworms. Fruit and berries. Wombaroo Small Carnivore Mix.
Orphaned young: OR	• Wombaroo >.7 Kangaroo Milk Replacer. • Di-Vetelact Low Lactose Animal Formula.

Planigale housing should include a base of soil and leaf litter landscaped with clumps of tussock grass, rocks, hollow branches and bark. These small marsupials can attack and eat prey larger than themselves. They differ from house mice in having teeth suitable for eating meat (page 140), four claws on the hind feet and either a pouch or pendulous scrotum.

Brush-tailed phascogales have a distinctive black tail and live in trees. Aggressive hunters, they pounce on spiders, centipedes, insects and occasionally small mammals and birds. Like other dasyurids they can be extremely vicious, and are best restrained by securing the head and supporting the body.

HOUSING

Large dasyurids should be housed in as big an aviary as possible. It should have metal frames covered with thick wire mesh because some animals can chew through thin wire netting and wooden frames. Grass or dirt floors are best, and put a wooden box in one corner for shelter.

Smaller species can be housed in a fish tank with a fine-wire-mesh lid for ventilation. Cover the base with loose soil, fine sand or leaf litter and place a nest-box in one corner. Try to provide a natural environment, with branches, logs, bark and dry leaves.

139

NATIVE RODENTS

The easiest way to tell rodents from marsupial "mice" (dasyurids) is by their teeth. Carnivorous marsupials have many upper and lower needle-like incisors and well-developed canine teeth. Rodents have two upper and two lower incisors which are long and curved, for gnawing. They have no canine teeth.

Unfortunately, most people are only aware of the introduced rodents often called vermin – house mice, and black and brown rats. But there are many species of native rodent, including water-rats, melomys, tree-rats, rock-rats, hopping-mice, bush rats and long-haired rats.

Due to their small size, native rodents (and small dasyurids) rarely come into care. They make a tasty meal for many other animals, so are more often relished than rescued.

Native rodents are predominantly herbivorous, but insects are eaten at times.

Natural food:	Native vegetation – new shoots, grass seeds, grasses, herbs, fruit, berries, roots and tubers. Water-rats are carnivorous and should be fed fish, yabbies, crayfish and large aquatic insects. Fresh water daily.
Supplementary food:	Aristopet Rat and Mouse Cubes. Aristopet Mouse and Rat Menu (selected seeds). Chopped fruit and vegetables.

CARNIVOROUS MARSUPIALS

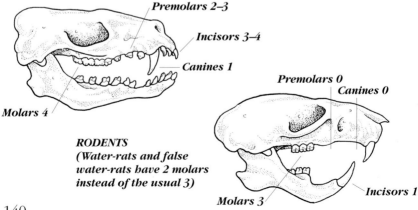

Premolars 2–3

Incisors 3–4

Canines 1

Premolars 0

Canines 0

Molars 4

RODENTS
(Water-rats and false
water-rats have 2 molars
instead of the usual 3)

Incisors 1

Molars 3

Unlike other native rodents, water-rats have dense, waterproof fur, partially webbed feet and are carnivorous, eating small fish, frogs, crustaceans and insects. It's difficult to distinguish native rodents from introduced species by their teeth alone, although the house mouse has notched upper incisors. Introduced black rats are excellent climbers often found in trees and roofs. They have large ears and eyes and a tail longer than their head-and-body length. Brown rats – also introduced – are poor climbers and are often found in sewers or cellars. They have small ears and eyes and a tail shorter than their head-and-body measurement.

HOUSING

Use a fish tank with a tight-fitting wire-mesh lid. Wooden or plastic housing is not suitable because rodents can gnaw through it and escape.

Line the base of the tank with fine sand, loose soil or leaf litter and provide a nest-box in one corner. Include natural features such as loose bark, logs and rocks.

141

APPENDIX

WILDLIFE AUTHORITIES

The following government bodies can assist you with enquiries regarding native wildlife, obtaining permits to keep protected species, permission to release native wildlife and contact phone numbers for local regional offices and wildlife organisations. As rules and regulations differ slightly in each State, it's important to contact the relevant wildlife authority before keeping native animals in captivity.

Australian Capital Territory
Compliance, Quarantine and Agistment Services
PO Box 1038, Tuggeranong, ACT 2901
Phone (02) 6207 6376

New South Wales
National Parks and Wildlife Service
43 Bridge Street, Hurstville
PO Box 1967, Hurstville, NSW 2220
Phone (02) 9585 6444

Northern Territory
Parks and Wildlife Commission
PO Box 496, Palmerston, NT 0831
Phone (08) 8999 4536

Queensland
Department of Environment
160 Ann Street, Brisbane
PO Box 155, Brisbane Albert Street, Qld 4002
Phone (07) 3227 8185

South Australia
Department of Environment and Natural Resources
GPO Box 1782, Adelaide, SA 5001
Phone (08) 8204 8700

Tasmania
Parks and Wildlife Service
134 Macquarie Street, Hobart
GPO Box 44A, Hobart, Tas. 7001
Phone (03) 6233 6556

Victoria
Department of Natural Resources and Environment
PO Box 41, East Melbourne, Vic. 3002
Phone (03) 9412 4011

Western Australia
Department of Conservation and Land Management
50 Hayman Road, Como, WA 6152
Phone (08) 9334 0333

COMMERCIAL PRODUCTS FOR WILDLIFE

Aristopet

Avi-vite – vitamin, amino acid and mineral supplement.
Avi-cal – calcium supplement.
Insecticidal dusting powder – to control lice and mites.
Bird mite and lice spray – low-toxicity spray.
Dry lorikeet diet – dry food mix.
Lorikeet and honeyeater – wet diet.
Premium birdseeds – assorted varieties available.
Egg and biscuit – rearing food for seed-eaters.
Rat and mouse pellets.
Mouse and rat menu – selected seeds.
Repti-cal – vitamin supplement for reptiles and frogs.

Manufacturer:	Aristopet
	35 Beeston Street
	Teneriffe, Qld 4005
	Ph: (07) 3254 2222
Suppliers:	Pet shops and produce stores.

Biolac

A leaflet outlining the use of these milk products and an approximate analysis of the nutrients the formulas contain is available on request.
M100 – early lactation milk.
M150 – mid-lactation milk for marsupials.
M200 – late lactation milk for marsupials.
M100-G – with Galacto-oligosaccharides for furless joeys.
Feeding bottles – 120 mL easy-to-clean bottles with printed graduated liquid measurements.
T1 Long joey teat – hard or soft.
T2 Long, fine teat – for very small orphans.
T3 Multi-purpose teat – for possums, wombats, koalas and flying-foxes.
T4 Short, fine teat – for small possums and gliders.

Manufacturer:	Biolac
	Geoff and Christine Smith
	PO Box 93
	Bonnyrigg, NSW 2177
	Ph: (02) 9823 9874
Supplier:	Contact Biolac.

Di-Vetelact

Di-Vetelact Low-lactose Animal Formula for rearing mammals.

Manufacturer: Sharpe Laboratories Pty Ltd
12 Hope Street
Ermington, NSW 2115
Ph: (02) 9858 5622

Suppliers: Pet shops, produce stores and veterinary clinics.

Roudybush

Formula 3 – handfeeding formula for seed-eating birds.
Squab Handfeeding Formula – for newly hatched pigeons and doves.
Maintenance Pellets and Crumbles – nutritionally balanced food for seed-eaters.

Manufacturer: Roudybush Australia
PO Box 831
Newcastle, NSW 2300
Ph: (02) 4954 5739

Suppliers: Pet shops, produce stores and veterinary clinics.

Vetafarm

Poly-aid – energy and protein supplement with multi-vitamins and electrolytes for sick/injured wildlife.
Soluvet – water-soluble vitamin supplement for birds and marsupials.
Calcivet – liquid calcium and vitamin D3 supplement for birds and reptiles.
Seabird Vitamin Tablets – vitamin supplement for seabirds being fed on frozen fish.
Golden Lori – natural liquid food blend for birds and small mammals.
Eureka – vitamin-and-mineral-enriched soft food for birds.
Handrearing food – soy-free handrearing formula for birds.
Crop needles – 8, 12, 14, 16 and 18 g – stainless steel.
Avian Insect Liquidator – to control external parasites on birds, mammals and reptiles.
Avi Safe – disinfectant cleanser effective against bacteria, viruses and fungi in animal environments.

Manufacturer: Vetafarm
3 Bye Street
Wagga Wagga, NSW 2650
Ph: (02) 6925 6222

Suppliers: Veterinary clinics and pet shops.

Wombaroo

Information booklets are available upon request. They contain detailed information on the use and nutritional content of various products, together with growth and feed estimates for many different species.

Insectivore Rearing Mix – for insect-, meat- and fish-eating birds.
Granivore Rearing Mix – for seed-eating birds.

Lorikeet and Honeyeater Food – for nectar-eating birds.
Small Carnivore Food – for insect- and meat-eating mammals.
Reptile Supplement – for tortoises, lizards and snakes.
High Protein Supplement – for fruit- and nectar-eating animals.
Kangaroo Milk Replacer – <.4, .4, .6, >.7 for all macropods.
Possum Milk Replacer – <.8, >.8 for possums and gliders.
Koala Milk Replacer – early, mid, late.
Wombat Milk Replacer – <.4, .4, >.6
Echidna Milk Replacer – <30 days, >30 days.
Flying-fox Milk Replacer.
Gamma-g – colostrum replacer.
Insectivorous Bat Milk Replacer.
Feeding bottles – 120 mL with graduations.
Heating pads – 10 watts, 260 x 360 mm.
Latex teats: FM – for out-of-pouch kangaroos, wombats, koalas.
              STM – for small, in-pouch kangaroos, wallabies, possums.
              MTM – for in-pouch kangaroos, wallabies, koalas.
              TM – for out-of-pouch kangaroos, wallabies.
              LD – for possums, wombats, koalas.
              SD – for possums, gliders.
              C – for carnivorous marsupials.
              F – for flying-foxes.
              P – for small, difficult-to-feed mammals.
Manufacturer: Wombaroo Food Products
                   PO Box 151
                   Glen Osmond, SA 5064
Suppliers: Veterinary clinics and pet shops.
State distributors to wildlife carers:
                   NSW: Helen's Fauna Nursing Service (02) 4465 1328
                   (also supplies glass syringes and feeding tubes)
                   Vic.: Quamby Wildlife Shelter (03) 5367 2171
                   Tas.: Underwoods Store (03) 6239 0241
                   Qld: Albion Veterinary Surgery (07) 3357 7849
                   SA and NT: Native Trading (08) 8277 7788
                   WA: West Coast Pet Supplies (08) 9453 2933

Glossary

altricial chick – a newly hatched bird, completely dependent on its parents for food, warmth and shelter.

arboreal – lives in trees.

arthropod – invertebrate with a segmented body and an exoskeleton.

carnivore – an animal that eats other animals.

carrion – decaying flesh of a dead animal.

cloaca – final outlet of the gut, urinary and reproductive tracts in marsupials, birds and reptiles.

crop – enlargement of the gullet in grain-eating birds where food is stored for digestion.

crustacean – generally hard-shelled animal that usually lives in water, e.g. crab, yabby, shrimp.

dasyurid – carnivorous marsupial, e.g. quoll, Tasmanian devil, antechinus, dunnart.

diurnal – active during the day.

drey – spherical nest of twigs and shredded bark constructed by ringtail possums.

echolocation – short pulses of ultrasound emitted or reflected as a means of locating food or navigating.

ecology – the relationship between the natural environment and the animals it sustains.

ectothermic – reliant on heat from an external source to regulate body temperature.

euthanasia – putting an animal to death painlessly.

exoskeleton – the tough, external covering of arthropods such as insects, spiders, centipedes and crustaceans.

feral – non-native, normally domesticated animal that lives and breeds in the wild.

folivore – leaf-eating animal.

frugivore – fruit-eating animal.

granivore – grain-eating animal.

grazer – grass-eating animal.

habitat – the specific place where an animal lives. It provides food, water and shelter for the animal.

herbivore – plant-eating animal.

herpetologist – person who studies reptiles and amphibians.

hibernate – become completely inactive, lowering the body temperature to just above that of the surrounding air.

honeydew – rich, sugary liquid excreted by aphids.

insectivore – insect-eating animal.
larva (plural larvae) – immature stage of an insect.
lerp – sweet, waxy insect secretion.
mammal – warm-blooded animal that feeds its young milk.
manna – sugary secretion found under the bark of trees, caused by insects such as borers.
marsupial – mammal that gives birth to very immature young that usually develop and grow inside a pouch.
migration – regular seasonal movement of animals from one area to another.
mollusc – soft-bodied animal with hard shell, such as snail, oyster, mussel.
monotreme – egg-laying mammal.
nectivore – nectar-eating animal.
nocturnal – active at night.
omnivore – eats both plant and animal food.
oocyst – microscopic cyst-like egg of a single-celled parasite such as coccidia.
placental mammal – mammal that gives birth to fully developed young that have grown attached to a placenta inside the uterus.
precocial chick – newly hatched bird that is covered in downy feathers, able to feed itself and move independently.
predator – animal that hunts others for food.
prehensile – able to grasp objects firmly.
prey – animal that is killed and eaten by another animal.
rodents – gnawing mammals such as rats.
scavenger – eats animals that are already dead.
slurry – thin liquid.
solitary – prefers to live alone.
sonar – see echolocation.
species – group of animals that share common characteristics and are capable of breeding with one another, producing fertile offspring.
terrestrial – lives on the ground.
torpid – sluggish and cold due to being in torpor.
torpor – brief state of inactivity due to cold or food shortage.
toxic – poisonous.
vent – external opening of the cloaca.

Bibliography

Australian Wildlife. Proceedings 104 (abridged 1994), Post Graduate Committee in Veterinary Science, University of Sydney, 1988.

Augee, M.L. and B. Gooden. *Echidnas of Australia and New Guinea*. University of NSW, Sydney, 1993.

Bat Lyssavirus Information. Australian Bird and Bat Banding Scheme of Environment Australia and the Communicable Diseases Network Australia New Zealand, GPO Box 9848, Canberra, ACT, 1996.

Bax, A. *Raising Native Frogs*. RANA, PO Box 310, Inala, Qld, 1996.

Cayley, N.W. *What Bird is That?* Angus & Robertson, North Ryde, NSW, 1987.

Cogger, H. *Reptiles and Amphibians of Australia*. Reed Books, NSW, 1996.

Collins, L. *Hand-rearing and Development of the Orphaned Flying-Fox*. Linda Collins, PO Box 436, Nimbin, NSW, 1995.

Dawson, T.J. *Kangaroo – The Biology of the Largest Marsupial*. University of NSW, Sydney, 1995.

Fauna. Proceedings 36, Post Graduate Committee in Veterinary Science, University of Sydney, 1978.

George, H. *Echidnas – Rescue Rehabilitation Release*. Helen George, 1255 Moss Vale Road, Beaumont, NSW, 1996.

George, H. *The Care & Handling of Orphaned Macropods*. Helen George, 1255 Moss Vale Road, Beaumont, NSW, 1988.

George, H. *The Hand-Rearing and Management of Captive Grey-Headed Flying-Foxes*. Helen George, 1255 Moss Vale Road, Beaumont, NSW, 1998.

George, H., G. Parker and P. Coote. *Common Wombats – Rescue Rehabilitation Release*. Helen George, 1255 Moss Vale Road, Beaumont, NSW, 1995.

Gow, G. *Graeme Gow's Complete Guide to Australian Snakes*. Cornstalk, Pymble, NSW, 1989.

Gow, G. *Snakes of Australia*. Angus & Robertson, North Ryde, NSW, 1986.

Grigg, G., J. Jarman and I. Hume (eds). *Kangaroos, Wallabies, Rat-Kangaroos*. Surrey Beatty, Chipping Norton, NSW, 1989.

Hand, S. *Care and Handling of Australian Native Animals*. Surrey Beatty, Chipping Norton, NSW, 1990.

Hanger, J. *Basic Reptile Care for Wildlife Volunteers*. Jon Hanger, WILDCARE, PO Box 2379, Nerang Mail Centre, Qld, 1997.

Hanger, J. *Diseases of Macropods for the Foster Carer*. Jon Hanger, WILDCARE, PO Box 2379, Nerang Mail Centre, Qld, 1997.

Hanger, J. *Principles of Koala Care for Volunteer Wildlife Carers*. Jon Hanger, WILDCARE, PO Box 2379, Nerang Mail Centre, Qld, 1997.

Henderson, N. *Australian Bird Rehabilitation Manual*. Norma Henderson, 49 Bakers Road, Church Point NSW, 1997.

Information for Public Health Authorities on Bat Lyssavirus. Lyssavirus Expert Group and Communicable Disease Network Australia New Zealand, GPO Box 9848, Canberra, ACT, 1996.

Kingsford, R. *Australian Waterbirds*. Kangaroo Press, Kenthurst, 1991.

Luckhoff, H. and T. Minogue. *A Gentle Method of Raising Orphaned Flying-Foxes.* ONARR, PO Box 3015, Darra, Qld, 1996.

Macdonald, J.D. *Birds of Australia.* Reed Books, Chatswood, NSW, 1984.

Macwhirter, P. (ed.). *Everybird – A Guide to Bird Health.* Inkata Press, Chatswood, NSW, 1994.

Markus, N. and N. Valzacchi. *Orphaned Flying Fox Hand-Raising Procedures.* Currumbin Sanctuary, 28 Tomewin Street, Currumbin, Qld, 1996.

McCracken, H. *Husbandry and Veterinary Care of Orphaned Marsupial Pouch Young.* Royal Melbourne Zoological Gardens, PO Box 74, Parkville, Vic., 1996.

Murray, E. *Living with Wildlife.* Reed Books, Frenchs Forest, NSW, 1989.

Parsons, H. *Bird Care – The Rehabilitation of Native Birds.* Heather Parsons, 20 Lindsay Avenue, Ermington, NSW, 1993.

Peters, C.A. *First Aid and Formulae for Feeding Sick, Injured and Baby Birds.* Bird Care and Conservation Society Inc., 120 Wakefield Street, Adelaide, 1992.

Phillips, B. *Koalas – The Little Australians We'd All Hate to Lose.* AGPS Press, Canberra, ACT, 1990.

Phillips, K. *Koalas – Australia's Ancient Ones.* Macmillan, New York, USA.

Reader's Digest Complete Book of Australian Birds. Reader's Digest, Surrey Hills, NSW, 1986.

Simpson, K. and N. Day. *Field Guide to the Birds of Australia.* Viking O'Neil, Ringwood, Vic., 1993.

Robinson, M. *A Field Guide to Frogs of Australia.* Reed Books, Chatswood, NSW, 1993.

Slater, P. *The Slater Field Guide to Australian Birds.* Rigby, Willoughby, NSW, 1986.

Smith, B. *Caring for Possums.* Kangaroo Press, Kenthurst, NSW, 1995.

Smith, A.P. and I.D. Hume (eds). *Possums and Gliders.* Surrey Beatty, Chipping Norton, NSW, 1996.

Stanvic, S. *Possums.* Sonya Stanvic, Blue Mountains WIRES, PO Box 146, Lawson, NSW, 1992.

Strahan, R. (ed.). *The Australian Museum Complete Book of Australian Mammals.* Angus & Robertson, North Ryde, NSW, 1983.

Strahan, R. (ed.). *The Mammals of Australia.* Reed Books, Chatswood, NSW, 1995.

Swanson, S. *Lizards of Australia.* Angus & Robertson, North Ryde, NSW, 1987.

Triggs, B.E. *The Wombat – Common Wombats in Australia.* University of NSW, Sydney, 1988.

Triggs, B. *Tracks, Scats and Other Traces.* Oxford University Press, South Melbourne, Vic., 1996.

Tyler, M.J. *Australian Frogs – A Natural History.* Reed Books, NSW, 1994.

Urban Wildlife. Proceedings 204, Post Graduate Committee in Veterinary Science, University of Sydney, 1992.

Walraven, E. *Rescue and Rehabilitation of Oiled Birds.* Taronga Zoo, Mosman, NSW, 1992.

Walraven, E. *Taronga Zoo's Guide to the Care of Urban Wildlife.* Allen and Unwin, North Sydney, NSW, 1990.

Weigel, J. *Care of Australian Reptiles in Captivity.* Reptile Keepers' Association, PO Box 227, Gosford, NSW, 1988.

Welfare of Kangaroos and Wallabies in Captivity. Macquarie University, North Ryde, NSW, 1995.

Wildlife. Proceedings 233, Post Graduate Committee in Veterinary Science, University of Sydney, 1994.